FISH SANDWICHES

The Delight of Receiving God's Promises

TROY SCHMIDT

NavPress

A NavPress resource published in alliance
with Tyndale House Publishers, Inc.

NavPress ◭

NavPress is the publishing ministry of The Navigators, an international Christian organization and leader in personal spiritual development. NavPress is committed to helping people grow spiritually and enjoy lives of meaning and hope through personal and group resources that are biblically rooted, culturally relevant, and highly practical.

For more information, visit www.NavPress.com.

Fish Sandwiches: The Delight of Receiving God's Promises

A NavPress resource published in alliance with Tyndale House Publishers, Inc.

NAVPRESS is a registered trademark of NavPress, The Navigators, Colorado Springs, CO. The NAVPRESS logo is a trademark of NavPress, The Navigators. *TYNDALE* is a registered trademark of Tyndale House Publishers, Inc. Absence of ° in connection with marks of NavPress or other parties does not indicate an absence of registration of those marks.

The Team:
Don Pape, Publisher
David Zimmerman, Acquisitions Editor
Elizabeth Symm, Copy Editor
Daniel Farrell, Designer

Cover photograph of fish sandwich copyright © Tanor/Shutterstock. All rights reserved.

Cover photograph of eaten sandwich by Thom King. Copyright © Tyndale House Publishers, Inc. All rights reserved.

Published in association with the literary agency WTA Services LLC, Franklin, TN.

Visit the author's website at www.reasonhope.com.

Some of the anecdotal illustrations in this book are true to life and are included with the permission of the persons involved. All other illustrations are composites of real situations, and any resemblance to people living or dead is purely coincidental.

For information about special discounts for bulk purchases, please contact Tyndale House Publishers at csresponse@tyndale.com, or call 1-800-323-9400.

Cataloging-in-Publication Data is available.

ISBN 978-1-63146-841-4

Printed in the United States of America

25	24	23	22	21	20	19
7	6	5	4	3	2	1

THANKS TO

Barbie, for feeding my heart every day

Riley, Audrey, Brady, Alana, Carson, and
Penelope, for filling me through your lives

First Baptist Church Windermere, for being
a church that serves love and grace

CONTENTS

#1 HUNGRY?:
What to Eat When Your Cupboard Is Bare *1*

#2 FEEDING THOUSANDS:
The Second-Greatest Miracle in the Bible *9*

#3 ATTENTION:
The Promise That God Knows Your Need *21*

#4 COMPASSION:
The Promise of God's Heart *35*

#5 BREAD, FISH, AND A BOY:
The Promise of Provision *51*

#6 LOOKING UP:
The Promise of Spiritual Health *67*

#7 MIRACLE:
The Promise of God's Power *85*

#8 GROUPS OF FIFTY:
The Promise of Community *105*

#9 SATISFIED:
The Promise of Fulfillment *119*

#10 LEFTOVERS:
The Promise of Blessing *137*

#11 BREAD OF LIFE:
The Promise of Eternity *161*

#12 COMMUNION:
"Take and Eat" *183*

The Feeding of the Five Thousand *187*
The Feeding of the Four Thousand *191*
Promises from the Scriptures *193*
Notes *205*

My soul is starved and hungry, ravenous!—
insatiable for your nourishing commands.

PSALM 119:20, *THE MESSAGE*

#1

HUNGRY?

What to Eat When Your Cupboard Is Bare

REMEMBER this nursery rhyme from childhood?

Old Mother Hubbard
Went to the cupboard
  To get her poor dog a bone;
But when she came there
The cupboard was bare,
  And so the poor dog had none.[1]

Some old lady goes to get her poor dog something to eat. She opens the drawers and finds nada, nothing, zilch—not even a piece of discarded marrow, the part people usually throw out.

The dog, sadly, must go hungry.

And the poor lady, too—unless, out of desperation, she must eat the . . .

No, let's not think such things.

How did she get into such a predicament? Did her social security run out? Did she make bad or overly enthusiastic investments in the stock market? Maybe Old Man Hubbard, who once provided a generous income, is now shacking up with one of the eight Maids a-Milking, leaving her with a stack of bills?

What does it matter? She's hungry. She needs to eat. Now.

Like Old Mother Hubbard, many of us find our cupboards empty these days, as a result of . . .

- recession
- unemployment
- job cutbacks
- bank collapses
- church collapses
- relationship collapses
- terrorism
- drought
- floods
- political upheaval
- stock market instability
- greed
- apathy
- war

Once, your cupboards stored delectable treats and important staples to your diet. Now, even the cockroaches have given up hope.

You may be hungry, but is food all you need? Moses reminded the Israelites of an important lesson about food that God taught them in the desert:

> He humbled you, causing you to hunger and then feeding you with manna, which neither you nor your ancestors had known, to teach you that man does not live on bread alone but on every word that comes from the mouth of the LORD.
>
> DEUTERONOMY 8:3

These words are so powerful that Jesus quoted them to Satan. Remember when Jesus fasted forty days in the wilderness and Satan came and tried to make him turn rocks into bread? Cool trick, right? But Jesus wouldn't fall for Satan's veiled attempt to control him.

Won't work. Ever. Satan doesn't call the shots or make the promises. Jesus does.

But let's face it: Jesus *was* hungry, and some nice Rocky Mountain bread sounded delicious. Yet Jesus fired back with the idea that while physical bodies need food, people need more than food.

SATAN DOESN'T CALL THE SHOTS OR MAKE THE PROMISES. JESUS DOES.

Jesus said to Satan, "Bread isn't the most important thing these physical bodies need. What they really need is God's Word."[2]

Food isn't always the solution to our needs. As Jesus and Deuteronomy 8:3 both state, *we need every word that comes from the mouth of the Lord.*

What good do words do when you're hungry? You've heard the expression "You're going to eat those words," which makes a seven-syllable snack sound good when you're starving. You'll eat anything, right? But words have no nutritional value to your body, so Jesus' direction must mean something else.

According to the verse in Deuteronomy, God sometimes causes physical hunger to teach **THE PROMISES** us to desire spiritual truths. He leads us out **OF GOD CAN'T BE** into the desert to show us what's really impor- **SEEN, BUT YOU** tant. He allows us to experience hard times so **CAN SEE THEM** we ask ourselves deeper questions about God. **WORKING.** Maybe that's what is happening to you right now.

So, what words from the mouth of the Lord sustain us when we are starving? Which words fill our souls with the most nutritional value? Which words are tastiest when life turns bitter?

The promises of God found in the Word of God.

The Israelites lived off a steady diet of promises that kept them alive during their desert days. Frankly, they had nothing else out there in the wilderness. God's promises provided protection and purification from the harsh, naked, unfertile elements. Everything they received came about as a direct promise from God.

Food . . .

Water . . .

Clothes . . .

Protection . . .

It works the same way today.

Many of those promises cannot be stacked in cupboards, but they are stored in our hearts. They can't be seen, but you can see them working. They can't be eaten, but they can be consumed into your life.

God's promises fill those empty spots in our hearts that food cannot touch. They make us feel blessed, full—even rich with a prosperity beyond money that goes deep into the very recesses of our souls.

And we see God feeding us those promises in a buffet Jesus served to a group of hungry people.

What was on the menu? Fish sandwiches.

You're blessed when you've lost it all.

God's kingdom is there for the finding.

You're blessed when you're ravenously hungry.

Then you're ready for the Messianic meal.

LUKE 6:20-21, *THE MESSAGE*

#2
FEEDING THOUSANDS
The Second-Greatest Miracle in the Bible

THE RESURRECTION was the most important miracle Jesus performed in the Bible. At that moment, Jesus overcame death by exiting the grave and proved that he was God. It's so important that all four Gospels talk about it.

So what's Jesus' second-greatest miracle based on Gospel coverage?

That's easy. The Feeding of the Five Thousand. Why? It, too, is recorded in all the Gospels. No other miracle besides those two is mentioned in all four.

Not walking on water.

Not healing the man born blind.

Not raising a little girl to life.

Feeding five thousand people at one time received more exposure than bringing Lazarus back from the dead. It was that big of a deal.

And get this: It was so amazing, there was a sequel—the Feeding of the Four Thousand.

So how do you feed five thousand hungry people all at once?

Easy: You make fish sandwiches.

Here's the recipe:

Bread + Fish = Fish Sandwich

This simple formula was the basis of the second-most important miracle in the history of the world.

So what happened during the feeding of the multiplied fish and bread that made it so noteworthy?

Let's take a look at what happened.

The Feeding of the Five Thousand

The scene occurred in northern Israel, near the Sea of Galilee.[1] The Jewish Passover was nearing. Many groupies were following Jesus because he performed such amazing miracles, and his teaching was like nothing they'd ever heard before.

It was late afternoon or early evening as Jesus and the disciples sat down on a mountainside, looking out over the thousands that had gathered. The disciples came to Jesus and said, "We stopped in a remote place, and these people need to eat. Tell them to take off, hit the local village, and grab some dinner."

Jesus listened to their request, then turned to Philip and said, "Why don't you feed them?"

Philip, caught off guard, looked perplexed. The others felt the same. "Us? It's going to take eight months' wages to feed all these people! Do we look like we have that kind of money?"

Jesus leaned back, smiling. He loved to test his followers, especially because he knew the answer. "How much food can you find right now?"

The disciples worked the crowd, asking if anyone had any food. Andrew, Simon Peter's brother, found a boy with five small barley loaves and two small fish. "This is all the food we can find. One kid was smart enough to bring his supper! That's not going to be enough."

"Sounds good," Jesus said, sitting up and extending his hands. "Give them to me."

The disciples handed over the paltry meal, not enough to feed even the thirteen of them.

Jesus motioned toward the crowd. "Have them sit in groups of fifty."

The disciples shrugged, then mingled through the thousands of people, telling them to gather in groups.

Jesus took the five loaves and held them to the sky. "Thank you, Father, for what you have provided and what you are going to do!" He broke the bread. Then he handed the pieces to the disciples.

And more pieces . . .

And more pieces . . .

And even more pieces . . .

More and more bread came out of nowhere.

Then Jesus did the same with the fish.

The astonished disciples delivered the food to the hungry groups. Thousands ate as much as they wanted—fish sandwiches for everyone!

When the people were full and satisfied, Jesus told the disciples to pick up all the leftovers. "I don't like anything going to waste."

They did, filling twelve baskets with the pieces that originated from those five barley loaves and two fish.

In the end, five thousand men were fed, not counting the women and children.

* * *

I had the opportunity to visit the area where some scholars believe this miracle occurred. My first stop took me to the Church of the Multiplication. Around the fourth century, a chapel was built to mark the spot many locals pointed to as the location of the Feeding of the Five Thousand. In the fifth century, a church was constructed on the same site. Invasions and wars leveled that original building; ancient mosaics from the church were excavated there, and the Church of the Multiplication was eventually rebuilt in its current form. The most famous mosaic from the Church of the Multiplication depicts a basket (with what looks like bread inside) and fish on each side of it.[2]

The church is near Tabgha, off the north/northwest corner of the Sea of Galilee. *Tabgha* comes from the Greek name *Heptapegon,* meaning "seven springs," and the village was frequented by fishermen because freshwater springs spilled into the Sea of Galilee, making it a popular hangout for fish.[3]

Nearby, you can find another church—the Church of the Primacy of Peter, a shrine that marks a possible location where the resurrected Jesus forgave Peter's betrayal.[4] This event happened while Peter and his men were fishing.

All this to say, the area was often frequented by Jesus. Just before Luke told the Feeding of the Fish Sandwiches story, he gave a clue to the location:

> When the apostles returned, they reported to Jesus what they had done. Then he took them with him and they withdrew by themselves to a town called Bethsaida.
>
> LUKE 9:10

Bethsaida and the Church of the Multiplication are very close, easily within walking distance for first-century people, who were accustomed to walking. The town's name means "house of fishing," just as Bethlehem means "house of bread."

Philip, Andrew, and Peter all came from Bethsaida (fish), while Jesus came from Bethlehem (bread).

Fish and bread. There's that theme again.

I went to the ruins of Bethsaida with Avner Goren, an Israeli archaeologist made famous by Bruce Feiler's excellent book and documentary *Walking the Bible*, to see the place where the miracle happened.

"Could Bethsaida have the resources to feed all these people?" I asked him, wondering if the disciples' request to have them all go into town to grab a bite would be at all possible.

Avner sat down on a stone wall, maybe once a home for someone who had been fed by Jesus himself that day. "This town only had a population of around five thousand."

There's that number again. What did it mean? I took a guess. "So Jesus could be saying there's enough of me to feed this whole town."

Avner nodded, ever the teacher, pleased the student was making the connection. "That's what it seems to be saying."

Five thousand is a lot of people. Facebook sets five thousand as its limit on the number of people it thinks you can know. Five thousand feels incredible, impossible, miraculous even to Mark Zuckerberg in our modern electronic age. But Jesus made five thousand friends in one day.

It gets better. Jesus fed even more than five thousand. Remember, the crowd counters in that day only counted the men. If you add women and children, that means Jesus may have fed *ten to fifteen thousand* at one time!

Take that, Facebook!

Feeding five-thousand-plus people all at once got so much press because it was too good to be true.

So, like any box office sensation, it got a sequel.

The Feeding of the Four Thousand

Some time after the feeding of the five thousand, Jesus and his disciples were walking along the Sea of Galilee when they came to another mountainside.[5] Word had gotten out that some "miracle guy" was in town, so people came and laid the handicapped, the blind, and those who couldn't hear or speak at the feet of Jesus, and he healed them. A huge party broke out, and everyone worshiped God.

Moved by the response, Jesus felt compassion for them. "We've been here for three days, and they have no food left. I've healed their bodies, but let's not starve them to death. Some of them traveled a long way and have to walk home. What do we have to eat?"

The disciples balked, but they knew the drill. They found seven loaves and a few small fish.

"Everyone needs to relax. Sit! Take a load off your feet!"

The crowd did exactly as Jesus asked.

The disciples found him in that familiar position, holding the bread and fish to the sky and thanking God. He broke them, just as before, and began handing them out to the disciples, piece by piece by piece by piece . . . until everyone was full of fish sandwiches.

In the end, seven basketfuls of broken pieces were left over.

This time, four thousand men ate, again not counting the women and children.

* * *

The amount of time that passed between the two miracles is unclear. The feedings in Matthew and Mark are separated by only a chapter or two, and while neither Gospel is known for its chronology, this literary-proximity factor would date them close to each other, anywhere between a couple of months to a year at most.

Avner took me to the place where some scholars believe the Feeding of the Four Thousand occurred. In Jewish life during Jesus' day, it was on the "other side of the tracks."

Kursi (or Gergesa/Gergesenes) sits on the eastern side of the Sea of Galilee. Bethsaida is easily visible across the sea. With its mountains and caves, the site has been venerated as the location where Jesus healed the man whose demons Jesus tossed into a herd of pigs. It was a Gentile, or non-Jewish, area—part of the Decapolis and today's Golan Heights. Wild pigs still roam there, and the caves along the shoreline would have acted as a burial ground in Jesus' time.[6]

So why mention this in context with the Feeding of the Four Thousand? How are the demoniac and the feeding of thousands tied together?

Matthew and Mark both tell the story of the demon-possessed man a couple of chapters before the Feeding of the Four Thousand. In the ruins of a Byzantine church (AD 500) marking the location of the healing of the demoniac, you can find another mosaic on the floor depicting fish and bread baskets. It reveals further evidence of Jesus' impact in this region. The Bible says the newly healed demoniac asked to join Jesus on his adventures, but Jesus told him to go home and tell everyone about his healing. He did, and that's the last we hear about him.

But it's interesting that when Jesus arrived in this Gentile territory the next time, Matthew and Mark say great crowds came to meet him. Why would great crowds of Gentiles come to meet Jesus? As non-Jews, they knew nothing of the prophecy of a coming Messiah. And Jesus didn't frequent the area. He had only stopped in once before that we know of. Jesus made it clear that he came for the "lost sheep of Israel"[7] and spent most of his time in Jewish territory.

Since the demoniac scene happened first, it's possible the man acted as Jesus' public-relations person, stirring up the region's fervor by showing off his miraculous mental healing. When Jesus dropped in a second time, crowds greeted the healer by bringing their own sick and handicapped people. If Jesus could cure the demoniac, surely he could cure others.

It's then, after the healing service, that Jesus fed a menu of fish sandwiches to those four thousand (plus) people on the guest list.

What's So Special about Fish Sandwiches?

All of Jesus' miracles were more than just miracles. They were messages, live-action parables to show us deeper truths about ourselves and God.

ALL OF JESUS' MIRACLES WERE MORE THAN JUST MIRACLES.

Jesus walked on water during a storm to show us that when life is rough, he'll meet us where we are and guide us to safe harbors.

He healed the blind man to reveal the truly blind people—the spiritual leaders of Israel.

Jesus healed the ten lepers to spotlight our need to appreciate what God does in our lives.

The Feeding of the Fish Sandwiches is no different. It's a miracle performed twice by Jesus, one of which (the Feeding of the Five Thousand) is recorded in all four Gospels. We should find much more insight into such a significant incident.

Surely these are not just stories about huge buffets but also spiritual signals about those things in life God wants to feed us when we're hungry. They reveal to us the heart of God. They fill us when we're hungry, comfort us when we're lonely, and fulfill us when we're unsatisfied.

They contain a buffet of promises that God wants to serve us:

- attention
- compassion
- provision
- spiritual health
- miraculous power
- community
- fulfillment
- blessing
- eternity

They give us everything we need when we're famished, alone, scared, confused.

Jesus answered, "It is written: 'Man shall not live on bread alone, but on every word that comes from the mouth of God.'"
MATTHEW 4:4

We need the promises of God found in the Word of God, displayed in the miraculous Feeding of the Fish Sandwiches.

Hungry? Let's dig in.

I'm GOD, your God, the very God
who rescued you from doom in Egypt,
Then fed you all you could eat,
filled your hungry stomachs.

PSALM 81:10, *THE MESSAGE*

#3

ATTENTION

The Promise That God Knows Your Need

*Jesus crossed to the far shore of the Sea of Galilee (that is, the Sea
of Tiberias), and a great crowd of people followed him because
they saw the signs he had performed by healing the sick. Then
Jesus went up on a mountainside and sat down with
his disciples. The Jewish Passover Festival was near.*

*When Jesus looked up and saw a great crowd coming toward him, he
said to Philip, "Where shall we buy bread for these people to eat?"*

JOHN 6:1-5

BARS. BARBERSHOPS. Coffeehouses. Diners. Pubs. What do all
these places have in common?

Psychologists call them *third spaces*, places away from home
or work where we interact with others on an informal level. In
1989, Ray Oldenburg published *The Great Good Place: Cafés,
Coffee Shops, Bookstores, Bars, Hair Salons, and Other Hangouts at
the Heart of a Community*, a book about this need for a place in
our lives where we're known on a different level. *Psychology Today*
says that according to the author,

Third spaces represent the heart of the community and
that such places are essential for social connectedness and
democracy. Third spaces provide stress-free, neutral spaces

for reconnection, renewal, and relaxation. According to Oldenburg, third spaces are "great good places," where people can gather on neutral ground to interact. These are places where people can put aside their concerns and enjoy good company and conversation in a space beyond the realms of home and work.[1]

TV sitcoms know third spaces very well. *Friends* has a coffee shop named Central Perk. Andy Griffith's town of Mayberry has Floyd's Barbershop. *Seinfeld* has the diner. The gang from *Cheers* has a bar, and a reason for their daily commitment to the establishment is found in the opening theme song:

> *Sometimes you want to go*
> *Where everybody knows your name,*
>   *and they're always glad you came.*[2]

Don't we all like to be around people who like us and who are like us?

People who know our names.

People who are glad we showed up.

People who can identify with us.

People who pay attention to us.

The Mexican restaurant chain Moe's Southwest Grill understands this. They rose in popularity because of their greeting when someone walks through the door: *"Welcome to Moe's!"*

It's also why Walmart stations greeters at the front door. They know it's easy to get lost inside their big store, so they make sure you feel noticed when you enter.

Retailers want you to know they are paying attention to you, not just with security cameras but also with face-to-face smiles and friendly, how-can-I-help-you attitudes. They want you to leave with a sense that you matter. If you think you matter, you will return as a loyal customer.

I'm a pastor at First Baptist Church Windermere, near Universal Studios and Disney World in Florida. We average around 1,800–2,000 on a Sunday, and my campus alone makes up about 1,000 of that number on Sunday morning. With three services on Sunday morning, it's a lot of people, and frankly, I don't know everyone's name. I wish everyone had to put on name tags when they walked in. I envy those who never forget a name and can call it up in a second. We have a church app that has saved me many times.

Yes, we want our churches to grow and for more people to hear the Good News, but there's an unfortunate side effect. As a church grows, people get lost in the crowd. I just got off the phone with someone whom I had not seen around for a while. I asked where she had been. Her answer?

"We left because nobody seemed to care whether we were there or not."

Many opt for smaller churches just to get that same experience Norm got when he walked into the *Cheers* bar.

"Norm!"

As one person in a world filled with more than seven billion people, each of us is hungry for attention.

I find some interesting trends that occur in people's Facebook statuses. They love to announce the most mundane things about their lives.

I went to Home Depot today.

I made this delicious sandwich.

My cat is funny.

People use social media as their "third space." It's become the bar, pub, bookshop, hair salon where we can post updates about our relationship statuses, political convictions, life philosophies, lunch plans, and pet antics—all in one place. From the monumental to the mundane, we want others to know everything that is going on in our lives. People crave attention, and clicking "Like" or "Love" or "Haha" or "Wow" lets someone know you see them.

God's Friends list contains seven-plus billion people, and he keeps up with them all day, all the time. He knows their statuses. Their birthdays. Their faces. He pays attention to where they went, what they had for lunch, and the hilarity of their cats. Everything.

He even knows what they look like and can rattle off their first, middle, and last names, including their high school nicknames and the names of all their children and grandchildren—which I can't do for any of my friends.

GOD PAYS BETTER ATTENTION TO OUR LIVES THAN WE DO.

God pays better attention to our lives than we do. Accurate, precise attention. That may be a tremendous source of comfort to you or a tremendous cause for fear, depending on what you're doing at the time.

In the Feeding of the Fish Sandwiches, we see God's attention focused on the people:

> When Jesus looked up and saw a great crowd coming toward him, he said to Philip, "Where shall we buy bread for these people to eat?"
> JOHN 6:5

In the midst of a chaotic mob scene, Jesus paid attention to the people's needs—both critical (urgent spiritual or physical issues) and common (the everyday experience of hunger).

God Pays Attention to Our Hunger

My stomach gets hungry during church. I don't know what it is about the 9:30 a.m. service. I could eat a Denny's Grand Slam Slugger breakfast and walk into church five minutes after sucking up the last of the syrup with a straw, and still my stomach would go *grrrrrrrrrr* during the sermon.

If I had been there for Jesus' Sermon on the Mount, people sitting around me would have missed certain portions of his speech because of my loud-mouthed food pit.

So embarrassing.

The universal sign for hunger is touching or rubbing the stomach. (There's also sticking your face into the Golden Corral all-you-can-eat buffet.) If you see someone doing this, you can bet they are hungry.

Great crowds of people swarmed Jesus everywhere he went. Many had needs—paralysis, blindness, seizures, missing appendages. The day he fed them fish sandwiches, Jesus looked at the crowd and said, "These people are hungry."

Hunger isn't the most obvious need when you look at a diseased and paralytic crowd, but it mattered to him.

How did Jesus know they were hungry?

Did a great, ominous stomach roar ripple through the crowd?

Did they all at once start patting their tummies?

Probably not. Jesus knew the current time and how long the crowds had been following him (plus, most likely, he got a hint from the Holy Spirit). Whether through logical deduction or spiritual insight, Jesus cared enough to pay attention to such a universal need.

In fact, Jesus thought about their hunger before they thought about their hunger. Nowhere in the accounts does it read that the people started complaining or asking about when the supper break would occur. Jesus looked ahead to their need and started thinking about ways to meet it.

IF HE KNOWS YOU'RE HUNGRY, JESUS LOOKS FOR A WAY TO FEED YOU.

God paid attention then, just as he does today. He knows about our bodies, our hunger clocks, our metabolism that burns different foods at different times of the day, depending on our activity.

You may have forgotten what you had for breakfast, but Jesus didn't. He knows what you had for dinner last night and the week before. These may not seem like significant details to you, but they are to God.

And if he knows you're hungry, Jesus looks for a way to feed you.

God Pays Attention to Our Hurts

No matter how cute of a name you attach to pain, kids react to a thin scratch as if it were an open head wound. Whether you call it a "boo-boo," an "ouchie," or an "owie," kids hate to get hurt.

Before their time in the desert, the Israelites cried out to their Father while the Egyptians persecuted them with slave labor.

During that long period, the king of Egypt died. The Israelites groaned in their slavery and cried out, and

their cry for help because of their slavery went up to
God. God heard their groaning and he remembered
his covenant with Abraham, with Isaac and with Jacob.
So God looked on the Israelites and was concerned
about them.
EXODUS 2:23-25

Later, as the Israelites escaped into the desert and struggled
with first hunger and, later, a monotonous diet of bread, bread,
bread . . .

The LORD said to Moses, "I have heard the grumbling
of the Israelites. Tell them, 'At twilight you will eat meat,
and in the morning you will be filled with bread. Then
you will know that I am the LORD your God.'"
EXODUS 16:11-12

The Israelites cried out to God in their painful slavery, and
God heard them. The Israelites cried out to God about food,
and God still heard them. No matter if the people's cry was out
of a real need or a petty want, God knew about their issue and
provided the resolution.

Throughout his ministry, Jesus stopped to help those in pain.
Some cried out to him from the streets. Others, he visited in
homes. One woman grabbed his cloak as he hurried off to bring
Jairus's daughter back from the dead. Even something as pressing
as healing a dying girl could not stop Jesus from paying attention
to a desperate woman suffering from bleeding.

If God's people are hurting, Jesus wants to know about it. He's
not too busy to stop and hear about your aches and pains. Jesus
knows about them, and he's hurting too.

God Pays Attention to Your Whole Life

I remember the fascination my wife and I had over our children while they were in the womb. Barbie's stomach would twist and roll as this unseen arm pressed against her flesh. Strange and wonderful times.

While for the most part I always came running after I heard cries of "He's moving," my day wasn't consumed with the second-by-second development of our gooey baby floating in amniotic fluid. My attention was sporadic, characterized by moments here or there.

Barbie was a different story. She carried the children with her, so the reminders were more prevalent. Her constant thoughts rested on this child just inches from her heart. She routinely prayed for each of our children.

In the same way, God constantly pays attention to our lives and our moment-by-moment growth and development.

> You created my inmost being;
>> you knit me together in my mother's womb.
> I praise you because I am fearfully and wonderfully made;
>> your works are wonderful,
>> I know that full well.
> My frame was not hidden from you
>> when I was made in the secret place,
>> when I was woven together in the depths of the earth.
> Your eyes saw my unformed body;
>> all the days ordained for me were written in your book
>> before one of them came to be.
> How precious to me are your thoughts, God!
>> How vast is the sum of them!

Were I to count them,
they would outnumber the grains of sand—
when I awake, I am still with you.

PSALM 139:13-18

Before we were born, God paid attention to us in a place only ultrasounds can see, even though we were a developing expansion of cells—a blob to the naked eye—not very attractive at first to anyone except the proud Father.

Now that we're all grown up, God still pays attention to us as if we were growing inside him, just inches from his heart.

He even has his eye on our future.

"For I know the plans I have for you," declares the LORD, "plans to prosper you and not to harm you, plans to give you hope and a future."

JEREMIAH 29:11

Every single moment of our lives—past, present, and future— God pays attention to us, carrying us, supplying us, and sending the Spirit to pray for us and direct us.[3] Not just parts of our lives, but our whole lives. He sees us not only as we are now but also how we were and how we are going to be.

God has a vast sum of thoughts, according to the psalmist, and they are directed at you!

The Promise That God Knows Your Need

Some time ago, in one of those rare father-son moments where hearts spill out over the fast food table, I asked my fifteen-year-old son Riley what he thought about dating, since his social calendar wasn't exactly filling up during those days. He took a thoughtful bite of a Thickburger, wiped his mouth on the back of his hand, and said, "It would be nice to know there is always someone out there thinking about you." At thirty years old, Riley is now married to that person (and also has a daughter to consume his own attention).

What he said was true—we all want to know someone is out there thinking about us.

That's God.

I cry out, hungry for attention, asking God if he cares, and I discover he's already caring about me.

God promises to pay attention not only to our needs now but also to our needs for the future.

Needs that we don't even have yet!

The very titles of God suggest this wonderful aspect of his nature.

A good King, he knows his subjects, loving and interacting with them.

As the Good Shepherd, he keeps a watchful eye on his sheep, making sure they are safe and leading them to greener pastures.

A Wonderful Counselor, he listens and responds to those who are hurting, offering suggestions for healing.

An Everlasting Father, he always loves his kids.

Jesus paid attention to the needs of thousands standing before him and in response served them fish sandwiches. Those fish sandwiches did more than address a hunger issue; they also addressed an intimacy issue. They were gifts of love showing the thousands that they were not alone—God was looking out for them.

This is a God who knows my name, who greets me when I walk in, who knows when I sit down, who keeps track of my bedtime, mealtime, and playtime, and who hears every concern I bring to him—big or small—whether now or in the future.

When you're alone, hurting, and wondering what to do next, it makes all the difference in the world to know someone is paying attention and still cares enough to invite you to dinner.

Saying Grace

Lord, thank you for the promise of your undivided attention. Thank you for seeing my hunger and my hurts. I'm humbled that you care enough to watch over me. Thank you for seeing me in the womb, making plans for me, and watching over my development and growth to maturity. You see all the needs I have now and those that lie ahead. You truly show your love to me by paying attention to my life.

He poured great draughts of water
down parched throats;
the starved and hungry got plenty to eat.

PSALM 107:9, *THE MESSAGE*

#4

COMPASSION
The Promise of God's Heart

*Jesus called his disciples to him and said, "I have compassion
for these people; they have already been with me three
days and have nothing to eat. I do not want to send them
away hungry, or they may collapse on the way."*

MATTHEW 15:32

CHANNEL FLIPPING produces guilt these days. Somewhere, on some
TV station, I always run across the same commercial. You've seen
it—the one with the starving children in a third world country.

My heart breaks as I see bloated stomachs and flies buzzing
around a toddler's mouth. I hear the call for only five dollars a
week to feed this poor, starving waif. So what do I do?

Nothing.

But wait, give me some credit—I reacted to the images, men-
tally assessing the children's situation, distantly feeling their pain,
even momentarily experiencing a physical response like a wince
or a guttural "Oh." Wasn't that enough?

Did I show sympathy? Yes. Sorrow? Sure. Compassion? No.

Why? Because compassion is heart.

Compassion means having a sense of sympathy or sorrow so

deep inside you that you want to do something to help the other person.

I like the term because it communicates more than just "I feel sorry for you"; it says "I hurt deeply for you, so what can I do to help?"

Here's the formula for compassion:

Sympathy + Action = Compassion

The apostle John addressed compassion in one of his letters to the churches:

> If anyone has material possessions and sees a brother or
> sister in need but has no pity on them, how can the love
> of God be in that person? Dear children, let us not love
> with words or speech but with actions and in truth.
> 1 JOHN 3:17-18

James, Jesus' half brother and author of a New Testament book,[1] also understood that compassion must include more than just sympathy.

> Suppose a brother or a sister is without clothes and
> daily food. If one of you says to them, "Go in peace;
> keep warm and well fed," but does nothing about their
> physical needs, what good is it?
> JAMES 2:15-16

When people share heavy prayer requests, most times I respond with a slow headshake and a sorrowful "Aww." That sound is meant to communicate my hurt for them. Yet that sound does nothing for the situation. That sound is not compassion.

God doesn't just "Aww" when we need him most. He shows compassion by helping us cope with the situation, finding solutions, and bringing resources to us, no matter what we're facing. God's heart for us motivates a clear response.

Before the actual Feeding of the Fish Sandwiches began, Jesus first paid attention to the need, and then his heart broke for the people. He didn't flip the channel, bothered by the hungry people before him. He said, "I have compassion for these people." It's a heartfelt emotion he revealed many times in the Gospels that brought about a reaction on his part.

So, who does God show compassion to today? God's heart is big enough to love seven billion people equally, and all at the same time. However, in the Bible, certain people get special focus because of their immediate needs. One of the following examples may be you right now.

God Shows Compassion to the Hungry and Sick

When Jesus landed and saw a large crowd, he had compassion on them and healed their sick.
MATTHEW 14:14

Jesus had compassion on them and touched their eyes. Immediately they received their sight and followed him.
MATTHEW 20:34

God's compassion extends out to the sick, the blind, the crippled, and even the hungry. During the Feeding of the Fish Sandwiches, Jesus' compassion stretched from a man in the crowd who needed a bite to eat to a man suffering with blindness. That's a wide capacity for compassion.

God sees the physical needs associated with all the suffering in our world, large and small, and he feels compassion for them all. But this question always arises: Why doesn't God feed all the hungry and heal all the sick today?

God does provide a means for feeding the hungry and curing the sick today.

Homeless shelters run by churches in cities all over the world feed and house thousands a day. Groups like Compassion International, World Vision, Samaritan's Purse, and Feeding Children Everywhere work tirelessly to bring food to the hungry. Our church packs around two hundred thousand meals a year for people in Burundi, a tiny African country that in 2014 was assessed as the hungriest nation in the world.[2]

Many hospitals were started by religious groups, and medical missionaries travel to remote parts of the world all the time. People are healed in a number of different ways through a number of different people. Clergy and deacons visit the sick daily and offer encouragement and prayer.

God asks the church to be the actively compassionate hands and feet that meet the needs of this world today.

Ultimately, God will demonstrate his final satisfying act of compassion by taking care of all our eternal needs in heaven.

Be patient. It's coming. In the meantime, the church does what it can to help the hungry and sick.

God Is Compassionate about the Poor, Widows, and Orphans

Using an electronic Bible, search for "widow+fatherless" (or "widow+orphan") and see that the terms frequently appear together. In Bible days, most people were poor, but the widows and orphans were the poorest of the poor. In the law he gave to Moses, God had put a welfare system in place called "gleaning":

> When you reap the harvest of your land, do not reap
> to the very edges of your field or gather the gleanings
> of your harvest. Leave them for the poor and for the
> foreigner residing among you. I am the LORD your God.
> LEVITICUS 23:22

God told the harvesters not to harvest everything in the field, but to leave the edges open and accessible to outsiders who needed it, so they could come by, pick a few bags of grain, and make their own bread.

The practice appears in the book of Ruth, when Ruth—a Moabite (non-Jew) widow—scoured the field and gleaned the extra grain. She understood what it was like being an outsider to the Jewish community, a poor widow separated from her family.

God felt compassion for people like her.

The poor, widows, and orphans are victims of situation. They're people who were dealt a bad hand in life due to the death of another, broken promises, bad decisions, or economic downturn.

Widows are widows because their husbands died or left them.

Orphans are orphans because their families died or left them.

The poor are poor because they cannot pay the bills or make ends meet.

While God feels for people's physical suffering, he's also compassionate about their situation as a whole, commanding the church to take care of them in their time of need.

> Religion that God our Father accepts as pure and
> faultless is this: to look after orphans and widows in
> their distress and to keep oneself from being polluted by
> the world.
> JAMES 1:27

I don't know what it's like being a widow or an orphan, but I have a pretty good grasp on being poor. I warned my wife during the proposal that she was marrying a starving writer. While we've never starved, we've seen bank accounts dwindle to starvation. We've faced serious financial crises. Three sons in college at once. A ballooning mortgage. A house diagnosed with termites. Medical bills from my wife's breast-cancer procedure.

One thing comforted me throughout: God felt for my economic situation. He knew about my pain, and I knew he was doing something about it.

God Is Compassionate about Outsiders

We know the nationality of the crowd in the Feeding of the Five Thousand.

> Jesus went up on a mountainside and sat down with his
> disciples. The Jewish Passover Festival was near.
> JOHN 6:3-4

These were "good" Jewish people who celebrated the Passover. Naturally, a Jew like Jesus would feel compassion for other Jews and their situation.

But what about the Feeding of the Four Thousand? Earlier, I explained that this miracle occurred on the eastern shore of the Sea of Galilee, in the region of the Decapolis.

Jesus is in a place both feared and hated by any "good" Jew—the land of the Gentiles. As we observed earlier, in modern terms this would be "the other side of the tracks," that area where those "not like us" live. You know the area. You have one nearby—where you roll up the car windows and lock the doors when you enter the territory. It's where the poor, violent, down-and-out, and out-of-work live. Only an organized mission trip would ever get you there.

Today, our bloodlines mix readily, and the popularity of blood tests like Ancestry DNA and 23andMe show we have more curiosity about our family trees. We celebrate our diversity, even brag about it. That was not the case in Jesus' day. Jews kept accurate genealogical records to make sure they stayed purely Jewish. They saw the world as either Jewish or not. Their term for the "not" is often translated as *Gentile*. Even if you were a half Jew, you were an outsider.

Samaritans were the outsiders of Jesus' day. The division between Jews and Samaritans went back to the days after King Solomon's death, when Israel divided after his son Rehoboam rose to power (around 930 BC). The ten northern tribes split from the southern tribes and started a nation whose capital eventually became Samaria. They built idols and worshiped other gods. God judged them by allowing the Assyrians to invade and scatter the inhabitants. Those Israelites married people from other countries, and their bloodlines mixed. They lost their purity.

Hundreds of years later, when Jesus visited Samaria during his travels and talked to a woman by a well, it was . . . unusual, even controversial. A Jew wouldn't stop and look a Samaritan in the eye. When Jesus told the parable about the Good Samaritan in Luke 10, the Jewish listener couldn't get past the oxymoron— Good . . . Samaritan?

Many scholars point out that the woman visited the well at

a time when most people didn't. John 4:6 points out that it was noon. Getting water was a morning task, when it was cooler, making the local well a gathering place to meet your neighbors and catch up on things.

This woman had a reputation for sleeping around. She went to the well at a time when people wouldn't be there to give her the stink eye, click their tongues, and turn their backs on her.

Among the outsiders, she was an outsider.

> The Samaritan woman said to him, "You are a Jew and I am a Samaritan woman. How can you ask me for a drink?" (For Jews do not associate with Samaritans.)
> JOHN 4:9

Yet Jesus stopped and talked to her. He acknowledged the division between their cultures and knew what kind of woman she was. But despite knowing all that, he took the time to answer her question and even referred to her five husbands later in their conversation.

> "Sir," the woman said, "I can see that you are a prophet. Our ancestors worshiped on this mountain, but you Jews claim that the place where we must worship is in Jerusalem."
> "Woman," Jesus replied, "believe me, a time is coming when you will worship the Father neither on this mountain nor in Jerusalem. You Samaritans worship what you do not know; we worship what we do know, for salvation is from the Jews. Yet a time is coming and has now come when the true worshipers will worship the Father in the Spirit and in truth, for

they are the kind of worshipers the Father seeks. God is spirit, and his worshipers must worship in the Spirit and in truth."

The woman said, "I know that Messiah" (called Christ) "is coming. When he comes, he will explain everything to us."

Then Jesus declared, "I, the one speaking to you— I am he."

JOHN 4:19-26

Jesus explained to her that he was the prophet the world was waiting for and that the true water of life, which this well could not offer her, was found in him.

An outsider among outsiders, and Jesus took the time to show her compassion.

Now imagine the Jewish disciples of Jesus standing before a crowd of four thousand Gentiles when suddenly, collectively, the stomachs of their enemies growled.

For a traditional Jew, the answer was "Let the outsiders starve to death. Serves them right for turning to other gods and starting those wars so many years ago."

For Jesus, the answer was "Feed them as if they were your own people; heal them as if they were your own brothers."

You may feel like an outsider or an outcast among your family, your friends, or your school. You may think nobody cares whether you live or die.

Not true. Someone cares for those living on society's borders of acceptance and rejection—God, who shows no favoritism.

And he's doing something to help you.

GOD SHOWS NO FAVORITISM. AND HE'S DOING SOMETHING TO HELP YOU.

God Is Compassionate about Sinners

In college, I had my first encounter with born-again Christians. I was your traditional college partier, tapping the keg after school on Friday and continuing until late Saturday night, then recovering all day Sunday. Church was out of the question. I didn't want to be a hypocrite, you know.

An evangelist named Jed Smock visited our college periodically with his sidekick, Sister Susan. The two stood in our square and pointed fingers at us, calling us "drunkards and fornicators." I had to ask someone what a fornicator was. Once I understood, I had to agree with their accusations. "Yep, they got that right. Drunkards and fornicators. That's us."

They presented God as angry and disappointed in us. A God who hated me and all my sins and couldn't wait to pass judgment on me. We all laughed and went on our way, drinking and fornicating.

They forgot to say that God's heart broke for us, and that in his compassion, he had done something sacrificial.

Even for the worst of us. Like this guy:

Ten years into my prison sentence . . . I was walking the prison yard on a cold winter's night. [Another inmate] introduced himself and began to tell me that Jesus Christ loved me and wanted to forgive me. Although I knew he meant well I mocked him because I did not think that God would ever forgive me. . . .

Still this man persisted and we became friends. His name was Rick and we would walk the yard together. Little by little he would share with me about his life and what he believed Jesus had done for him. He kept reminding me that no matter what a person did, Christ stood ready to forgive if that individual would be willing to turn from the bad things they were doing and would put their full faith and trust in Jesus Christ. . . .

He gave me a Gideon's Pocket Testament and asked me to read the Psalms. I did. . . .

One night, I was reading Psalm 34. I came upon the 6th verse, which says, "this poor man cried, and the Lord heard him, and saved him from all his troubles." . . .

I began to pour out my heart to God. . . .

I told Him that I was sick and tired of doing evil. I asked Jesus to forgive me for all my sins. I spent a good while on my knees praying to Him.

When I got up it felt as if a very heavy but invisible chain that had been around me for so many years was broken. A peace flooded over me. I did not understand what was happening. But in my heart I just knew that my life, somehow, was going to be different.[3]

The prisoner who wrote this is David Berkowitz—known as "the Son of Sam," a Satan worshiper who tormented New York City from 1976 to 1977, killing six people. He was given a 365-year prison sentence.[4]

God loves convicted killers like David Berkowitz? Many have a hard time with this thought, but the answer is *yes*. God's compassion is so great that it includes everyone, even those sinners fully hated and despised by this world. God even came to David Berkowitz in prison!

Jesus felt so much compassion for sinners that he risked his reputation and ate with them:

Now the tax collectors and sinners were all gathering around to hear Jesus. But the Pharisees and the teachers of the law muttered, "This man welcomes sinners and eats with them."
LUKE 15:1-2

At his crucifixion, Jesus hung on the cross between two sinners—convicted criminals, outsiders whom the Roman government wanted to get rid of. And yet Jesus literally reached out his hand to each of them—one who mocked him and one who accepted him.

YOU CAN NEVER GET SO FAR OUTSIDE GOD'S COMPASSION THAT HIS HEART CAN'T REACH YOU.

Then he said, "Jesus, remember me when you come into your kingdom."
Jesus answered him, "Truly I tell you, today you will be with me in paradise."
LUKE 23:42-43

God's compassion toward sinners—and that means every one of us—is seen in salvation. The Cross is the ultimate act of compassion, reaching out to all those on the fringes of society.

The Promise of God's Heart

How wide is God's compassion?

- The hungry and sick: those with physical needs
- The poor, widows, and orphans: those with situational hurdles

- The outsiders: those facing prejudicial hatred or rejection
- The sinners: those considered unrighteous

If we fall into any of these categories, we know that God sees our situations, that his heart breaks for us, and that he's moved to do something to relieve our pain—no matter what we've done, no matter who we are.

You can never get so far outside God's compassion that his heart can't reach you.

So this fish sandwich is for those on the fringe—the forgotten, the despised, and the lost. God sees you, and he's doing whatever it takes to reach out and help.

Saying Grace

Lord, thank you for extending your heart to me. Thank you for keeping my situation close to you and giving me the strength of your presence. Lord, whether I am hungry, sick, poor, forgotten, an outsider, or an insider, you not only feel for me but are also doing something to help. I can only overcome my situation because of your compassion.

The lines of purpose in your lives never
grow slack, tightly tied as they are to your
future in heaven, kept taut by hope.
The Message is as true among you today as when
you first heard it. It doesn't diminish or weaken
over time. It's the same all over the world. The
Message bears fruit and gets larger and stronger,
just as it has in you. From the very first day
you heard and recognized the truth of what
God is doing, you've been hungry for more.

COLOSSIANS 1:5-6, *THE MESSAGE*

BREAD, FISH, AND A E

The Promise of Provision

> When Jesus looked up and saw a great crowd coming
> toward him, he said to Philip, "Where shall we buy brea
> for these people to eat?" He asked this only to test him, f
> he already had in mind what he was going to do.
>
> Philip answered him, "It would take more than half a year's
> to buy enough bread for each one to have a bite!"
>
> Another of his disciples, Andrew, Simon Peter's brother, spo
> "Here is a boy with five small barley loaves and two small
> but how far will they go among so many?"

JOHN 6:5-9

I REMEMBER the absolute poorest time in my life. Durin
days in Los Angeles, I worked every chance I got, takin
that included everything from being a production as
movies and music videos to working at a movie theater
ing Jacuzzis in people's backyards. I saved money, clippe
and kept my overhead to a minimum. Besides rent and a
ance (I paid cash for a broken-down Oldsmobile Starfire
other monthly bill I had was a school loan I promised r
I would pay back. That monthly payment came to $58

As much as I cut back and scraped by, I found myse
one period of time, closing in on zero dollars in my

51

ccount and no money in savings. Work had slowed down con-
iderably, with nothing on the horizon.

I recently had become a Christian, and I began studying the
promises of God. I remember hearing, though I could never
quote you the verse at the time, that God would provide for me
when I needed him. That's all I knew. The pastor emphasized it
over and over, and we even turned to the passage in the Bible. It
was there. I knew it. Somewhere . . .

The school-loan payment deadline approached, and guess how
much I had in my balance when I opened my checkbook: $58.20.

A coincidence? I think not.

I was at a crossroads. Did I really believe this promise from
God? I mean, *really*? This was the moment of truth.

Did I have enough faith to allow my bank account to go to
nothing and trust God to produce something?

After a short prayer and a deep breath, I pulled out my pen
and wrote the check, bringing my balance to zero. I officially
had no money. I risked it all by paying a school loan. Fifty-eight
dollars buys a lot of ramen noodles. Of all the bills, I could
certainly miss one loan payment without serious damage to my
already-weak credit rating. The school-loan people would understand. Do they really expect you to pay those school loans back,
anyway?

But God said he would take care of me, and I wanted to see
if it was true. I didn't know how he would do it or where the
provision would come from, but I believed he had the resources.

Now you would expect as a reward for my leap of faith a big
refund check showing up in the mail or a disoriented millionaire
wandering around on the highway and handing me a fat wad of
money after giving him a lift to his house. No such thing. But
God did give me an idea.

I began a campaign called "Spare Change for Troy." I took an empty soup can, wrote the name of the campaign on the side, and went door-to-door in my apartment building with my plea. I approached everyone I knew and asked them to give me their change. After a few days, I had made . . . fifty-eight dollars. No joke.

Because of my desperate plea, I managed to find a couple of jobs in the process. Neighbors hired me for day jobs at their places of employment. Slowly but surely, the funds reappeared, and bankruptcy was never declared.

I have needed this faith to get by throughout my life. I lost a job months before my wedding, curtailing our original honeymoon plans. We got pregnant three months into our marriage, having our firstborn one week before our first anniversary. A year after his birth, we decided that my wife, Barbie, needed to leave her job at ABC Television to stay home and be a full-time mother, drastically cutting our income by well over half (she made more money than me). Three other couples and ourselves, all newlyweds with no money, formed a group called "The Poor Club." We gathered and found the cheapest things to do. Admission into the club was an *Entertainment* coupon book, packed with two-for-one and half-off deals.

But we never went hungry, and we never were homeless. The resources came when we needed them, and God has always kept his promises to us.

Jesus paid attention to the needs of the people gathered by the shoreline. He felt compassion for them, and now he needed to find provisions to meet the needs of the hungry. So Jesus turned to his disciples and challenged them. "Where are we going to get the resources to feed thousands of people?"

The disciples looked to their bank accounts (aka their pockets). Empty.

They turned to each other. "We don't have enough money between us to feed them!"

They calculated the approximate cost to feed everyone—eight months' wages.[1]

So how much is eight months' wages for you? Take your yearly salary, multiply it by .67 (eight months out of twelve), and imagine Jesus saying, "Feed all those people RIGHT NOW!" If you make a yearly salary of $50,000, that's $33,000 for fully catered box suppers. Yeah, right! Is there any way we can winnow that price down? How about one Tic Tac per person?

You see why it seemed impossible to feed all of them with the resources in their hands. But don't attack the disciples because of their lack of faith. We panic when we have fifteen guests coming over for dinner. Imagine opening the door and finding fifteen thousand hungry mouths.

HE HAS EVERYTHING WE NEED, EVEN IF IT MAY NOT SEEM THAT WAY AT FIRST.

We worry when we look at ourselves, our families, our checkbooks, and our refrigerators, wondering how we're going to feed five mouths for five days.

God's provision during the mass feeding included three very limited things: fish, bread, and a boy. Doesn't seem like much, but in God's eyes, it was all he needed.

At times like this, we acknowledge our limited resources and God's unlimited ability. He has everything we need, even if it may not seem that way at first.

The Fish: God's Provision Is Practical

Today around the Sea of Galilee, you can find lots of restaurants, especially in neighborhoods called kibbutzim (a sort of commune where everyone works and all needs are provided for).

Guess what item you find on the menu everywhere you go?

Fish. The tourist name is Saint Peter's fish, but you would know it as tilapia.

In the story of the fish sandwiches, Jesus fed the crowds a food they were very familiar with. They lived around it, had plenty of it, and probably ate it daily.

So why didn't Jesus surprise them with something different?

Maybe a penne pasta salad, ratatouille, or pad thai. Or a T-bone steak, fried potatoes, and corn on the cob with apple pie. What about a dessert like tiramisu, death-by-chocolate cake, strawberry-rhubarb pie, or a banana split?

Sorry. All he served was fish. It was a staple of their daily diets, so it was good enough for the moment. Jesus took what they needed and provided them with more of what they needed. No fancy French dinner or exotic Caribbean fare—just a common, everyday meal.

Open your refrigerator, and what do you see? Eggs, milk, ketchup, mustard, bread, some fruit and veggies, right? No pheasant under glass; no caviar; no coq au vin . . . at least not on a regular basis. Just the basics.

During my "Spare Change" campaign, God didn't drop a lottery ticket worth eighty-five million dollars on my lap. He provided the practical amount of what I needed to get by.

Over time, I found that once-vague verse that clearly promised me God's provision during desperate times. It's Jesus' most famous statement to the hungry, homeless, hurting, and needy:

> I tell you, do not worry about your life, what you will eat or drink; or about your body, what you will wear.

Is not life more than food, and the body more than clothes? Look at the birds of the air; they do not sow or reap or store away in barns, and yet your heavenly Father feeds them. Are you not much more valuable than they? Can any one of you by worrying add a single hour to your life?

And why do you worry about clothes? See how the flowers of the field grow. They do not labor or spin. Yet I tell you that not even Solomon in all his splendor was dressed like one of these. If that is how God clothes the grass of the field, which is here today and tomorrow is thrown into the fire, will he not much more clothe you—you of little faith? So do not worry, saying, "What shall we eat?" or "What shall we drink?" or "What shall we wear?" For the pagans run after all these things, and your heavenly Father knows that you need them. But seek first his kingdom and his righteousness, and all these things will be given to you as well. Therefore do not worry about tomorrow, for tomorrow will worry about itself. Each day has enough trouble of its own.

MATTHEW 6:25-34

God says, "If I provide for birds, grass, and flowers, why wouldn't I feed and clothe my people, whom I love far more?"

How does he show his love to the birds and flowers? The birds get worms and bugs. The flowers get sunshine and rain. The birds don't get Amazonian soil–raised organic worms, and the flowers don't get purified glacier water from Alaska. Just worms and water. Nothing fancy.

So how does God show his love to us? Food, drink, and clothes. The basics. No exquisite delicacies or overpriced water or the latest fashions from Paris. The world seeks after this kind of stuff because they think it's what life is all about. Jesus promises us the practical necessities of survival.

Not that he doesn't surprise us at times with gift certificates to restaurants we could never afford. It's just not what he promises on a regular basis.

I cannot demand Swiss steak, sweet potato enchiladas, fresh mozzarella with basil, or chocolate-berry cobbler to eat; or French champagne, Starbucks, or an acai smoothie to drink; or Yves Saint Laurent, Versace, Ralph Lauren, or Giorgio Armani clothes to wear. We need practical resources like eggs, peanut butter, mustard, bread, fruit, veggies, water, juice, milk. Nothing exotic, but enough.

If you need a car, God won't necessarily provide a Lexus. A '71 Chevy with missing hubcaps will get you where you need to go.

If you need a place to stay, God won't necessarily open up a bungalow for you at the Beverly Hills Hotel. Maybe crashing on a friend's floor or couch will do . . . for now.

If you need something to eat, God won't necessarily reserve a table for you at Ruth's Chris Steak House. Maybe the wind will blow a five-dollar bill to your feet outside Taco Bell.

Imagine a guy standing up in the ninety-eighth row of the Feeding of the Fish Sandwiches and shouting, "That's nice, but do you have any grilled lamb and rye bread?"

Standing in the wilderness without food in his pockets and this guy places a special order? He missed the point.

We had a woman and her child enter our church looking for money and some food. We so happened to have a pantry filled with many nonperishable items: mac and cheese, soups, noodles, jars of sauces. The woman looked at the food, shook her head, and said, "Do you have anything else?" She, too, missed the point.

God had provided for her, but it wasn't to her taste. Is that the time to question taste, when your child is hungry?

Thank God for a very practical promise to provide very practical resources to meet your very practical needs.

The Bread: God's Provision Sometimes Transcends Time and Space

Everybody eats bread in the movies.

Watch any movie or TV show with a character returning from the store, and you will always see a long, thin loaf of Italian bread sticking out of the bag. I'm not kidding. Test me on this.

Bread is easy to buy. Today, we push our four-wheel, deluxe shopping carts rigged with GPS mapping systems to find our way around fifty-aisled super-duper megastores; turn down the bread aisles, which could double as landing strips for B-1 bombers; carefully place the soft loaves of bread into our carts; then head to the checkouts, where baggers pile ten cans of clam chowder on top of them.

Back in biblical times, bread took a lot of effort to make. The wheat was harvested, then threshed and beaten to separate the kernels from the stalks. The stalks were winnowed with a fork (or rake), tossed, and blown away by the wind. The wheat kernels that fell to the ground were then sifted, removing rocks and impurities. What was left was finely ground with a stone and mixed with water or olive oil. The bread maker then added a piece of fermented dough called leaven, which acted as the rising agent. This leaven came from a previous batch and was made with white bran or barley. Mixed with water, it soured over time, then was added to the next freshly made loaf. Once everything was all mixed together, the bread maker patted the dough into flat pancakes and placed them on hot rocks on the fire.

The whole process took a day to finish. Quite a difference from our bread aisles that could feed five thousand people in a second.

That's what makes the Feeding of the Fish Sandwiches so amazing. Jesus somehow harvested, winnowed, and ground the wheat; stirred together the ingredients; then baked the loaves of bread in a matter of a second.

To bake enough bread for thousands, Jesus would need a week. Even gathering enough fish would take one hundred completely full nets.[2]

He didn't have that kind of time. People were hungry *now*! So to meet the need, Jesus transcended time and space. He was not limited to the time needed to bake and fish. He was not limited to the size of the barley field or the width of the net.

While sometimes providing our resources practically, he also does so miraculously, providing incredible abundance in impossible ways. He has the power.

At Creation, God spoke and stars appeared. He spoke and animals roared to life. If God wants something, he speaks it into existence instantaneously.

God isn't worried about the steps required to supply your needs. He isn't flustered, wondering how he's going to provide for you. I try so hard, during my times of poverty, to give God a detailed plan on how to get me what I need. I let him know what job to get me, when it should start, how much I should make, where I need to go.

I'm just saving God some time, right? He's a busy guy!

I forget that everything can change in a second if God wants it to happen.

I've seen this occur too many times.

Checks that arrive in the mail.

Jobs that come from out of nowhere.

Past acquaintances who remember me at the right time and call with a work request.

> **WHEN WE HAVE A NEED, WE NEED NOT WORRY ABOUT HOW GOD WILL PROVIDE IT. HE LAUGHS AT TIME AND SPACE.**

Church members at the door with food.

When we have a need, we need not worry about how God will provide it. He laughs at time and space.

It's always possible that he will do the impossible.

The Boy: God Asks Us to Surrender Our Own Provisions to Provide for Others

Car engines are my mortal enemy. If I'm standing on the side of the road, holding a screwdriver in front of my smoking car, and a mechanic walks up with the power to fix it, how can anything get done if I hold on to the screwdriver? I must release it into his capable hands.

> Another of his disciples, Andrew, Simon Peter's brother, spoke up, "Here is a boy with five small barley loaves and two small fish, but how far will they go among so many?"
> JOHN 6:8-9

Only John mentions the provider of the resources for the fish sandwiches . . . a small boy. The five loaves of bread and two fish did not come from the disciples' pockets, but from a young bystander, the only person smart enough to pack a supper for the road.

Five loaves and two fish can last one person a long time. It's a very satisfying meal. Why would the boy give it up?

First of all, Jesus requested it:

"We have here only five loaves of bread and two fish,"
they answered.

"Bring them here to me," he said.

MATTHEW 14:17-18

Being an obedient Jewish boy, he obeyed his elders. He gave them his food without requiring an explanation. Smart kid.

The boy released all his resources and placed them in the capable hands of Jesus and his disciples. He began the process of giving to others by giving to Jesus first. So what did the boy get in return? How did Jesus provide for him?

For starters, the boy got more bread and fish than he could ever imagine! But he got more than just food.

Imagine the boy's face as he watched thousands of fish and loaves of bread pouring out into the crowd, passed from hand to hand. Imagine as the boy stood in awe while men, women, and children laughed and ate, celebrating God and his bounty. A hillside party broke out, and they had a boy to thank. While many probably did not know about his sacrifice, the boy experienced the multiplication of his simple gift.

The process of giving our resources to Jesus is a release of all rights, results, ability, and ownership. It is a confession of our weaknesses and an acknowledgment of God's strength:

Lord, all I have here is yours. You do with it whatever you want. It's not much, but in your hands, I know it is a lot.

If we cannot turn over what little resources we have, it will be difficult to manage the many resources he can produce. The key here is faith, giving to God what is limited in your possession.

If that one boy had held on to his resources, fifteen thousand people would have gone unfed—the second-greatest miracle in the Bible thwarted by the stubbornness of one little brat who would not release his supper to Christ. It's tough to give up everything you have. In some ways, it doesn't make sense to say . . .

"We need food, and we only have a few cans of soup here, so let's give them to Christ."

"I have no time except for a few hours a week, so I'll give that to God."

"My checking account is low and I need to pay bills, so I'll start by giving to the church first."

Ridiculous? Seems so at first, but it's actually the wisest choice you can ever make. God has provided for you; now provide for others. The boy surrendered all his fish sandwiches to Christ and received not only a satisfying supper in return but also the satisfaction of blessing thousands in the meantime.

YOU CAN'T RECEIVE IF YOUR HANDS ARE FULL.

Give what you have to God. Put it in his hands. Honor him by showing your trust, love, and faith. He has so much more to give back to you. You can't receive it if your hands are full.

The Promise of God's Provision

This is not a give-to-get mentality. This promise does not scream of expectation. It cannot demand.

Through the fish-sandwich incident, God provided for everyone's needs through bread, fish, and a boy—resources that were practical and tangible. The people received the food without complaining. No special orders. They ate what they were given.

We also see that we must hold on loosely to the resources we are given so that we can be the means of providing resources for others.

Jesus easily could have produced the first fish sandwich out of thin air. He didn't need the boy's bread and fish as a catalyst. However, he wanted to teach an important lesson about giving, so he involved the boy in the blessing.

The boy gave up his supper, and all he was handed was another supper, but he witnessed thousands more getting something to eat too. The return on his giving was spiritual blessing, not monetary dividends.

God runs the warehouse of unlimited resources, and he can get you whatever you need, whether it materializes out of thin air or through a little boy with a giving heart.

Saying Grace

Thank you, Lord, for providing what I need. Keep me focused on what is practical and necessary, not on what is impractical and unnecessary. I rest knowing that no barrier keeps you from getting me anything. In the meantime, I must hold what I have loosely, knowing that you may ask me to surrender something to someone else in need. My resources are from you, for you to do with as you please.

You serve me a six-course dinner
right in front of my enemies.
You revive my drooping head;
my cup brims with blessing.

PSALM 23:5, *THE MESSAGE*

LOOKING UP

The Promise of Spiritual Health

Taking the five loaves and the two fish and looking up to heaven . . .

MARK 6:41

DON'T YOU LOVE peeking into people's carts when you shop? You can tell a lot about them by their items.

- Plenty of adult beverages and chips and salsa—partier
- Fourteen TV dinners and six boxes of Hot Pockets—bachelor
- Alfalfa sprouts, spinach, and low-fat vinaigrette—health nut
- Klondike Bars, Ghirardelli chocolate sauce, and potato chips—pregnant woman

I've also realized something else when shopping: Food that is good for you is expensive, and food that is bad for you is cheap. As I walk into a grocery store, I ask myself two questions:

1. What is good for me?
2. What can I afford?

Usually, finances override health. I wish it weren't that way, but situations force me to eat what the world market serves at bargain prices.

Away from the supermarket, we are also offered two choices in our lives—one by God and the other by the world. These choices have different nutritional values, determining our spiritual health. These choices come at different costs—some temporary, some eternal.

We need to make sure we consume what's best for us and stay away from what's bad for us.

I usually do that in the stores by reading labels. You will find me in the aisles holding up boxes, squinting at the fine print to check the ingredients, trying to pronounce names only chemists appreciate. I want to look at what I'm putting into my body.

In three of the four Gospel accounts of the Feeding of the Five Thousand, the writer says that Jesus took the bread and fish and *looked* up to heaven.[1] It's an interesting gesture, a pause in the action for only the slightest moment as Jesus stopped to consider the elements in his hand. There's no dialogue; just a thought, a glance to his Father. It was a moment of prayer, of consideration, making sure the food in his hands was okay, getting approval that they were the ingredients of God's will.

Jesus wanted to "check out" and receive confirmation from God before the miracle exploded.

God also promises the best for us, revealed in his will for our lives.

As we are given opportunities, we need to stop and hold our

choices up to God too, shopping and comparing them to make sure they are God's will and not the will of the world.

Are you willing to let God look into your shopping cart? Are you ready to follow his plan for your life?

Then start by looking up—not down.

Junk Food

As good as chips, cookies, and cakes taste, I have to break some bad news to you—they have very little nutritional value. A little bite here and there won't kill you, but a steady diet of Little Debbie cakes, Honey BBQ Fritos, and Twinkies will.

Junk food should be called *obscene food*. When we curse, we utter words that we don't need to say or that don't help our cause. In fact, we represent a curse word with random symbols that mean absolutely nothing, like this: @#!%*$. Cartoonist Mort Walker of *Beetle Bailey* fame called that string of symbols a *grawlix*.[2]

That's what junk food is. @#!%*$. Obscene.

Read the labels of junk foods: Preservatives, flavor enhancers, sugar substitutes, fat reducers—you might as well down a beaker of chemicals. Disgusting. Nutritionally obscene.

Junk food tastes good and looks good, but it's not good.

Life serves us junk food too: stuff that's obscene, makes us fat, and weighs us down. When we think it will satisfy our cravings, we turn to worldly junk food—things like worry, alcohol, pornography, drugs, material items, and work—to help us feel better. They never do.

Instead of looking up to God, we look down at the world for help and hope.

During the most difficult periods in my life, I tend to dine on worry. Worry about finances. Worry about family members. Worry about the future. Worry about the present.

I purchase worry in bulk, and a bountiful supply of worry is always in arm's reach. I fill my hands with it, shoveling it into my mouth. I bake worry slowly at 350 degrees for two hours, or I grill it up in searing heat until it's nice and crispy. I purchase a Crock-Pot so I can simmer my worry all day, even overnight, so that in the morning it's hot and ready to go.

Worry is my spiritual junk food. It sort of tastes good, kind of feels good for a little while—but it's not good for me at all.

Worry only adds unnecessary weight to my life, weight God promises to carry for me instead. Worry stresses my heart and leads to an early death.

Worry is junk because it looks to the world to find some relief. In the spiritual marketplace, we throw bags of junk food into our carts as we walk down the aisles of life. Instead of dining on God's best, we seek out those items that taste good for a moment, then leave us hungry minutes later.

> *WORRY IS SPIRITUAL JUNK FOOD. IT SORT OF TASTES GOOD, KIND OF FEELS GOOD FOR A LITTLE WHILE—BUT IT'S NOT GOOD AT ALL.*

What is that junk food? Sin. We know we shouldn't consume it. We know there are better choices, but man, it looks so good at the time.

Junk food changes as the world changes its tastes. We must consume more to keep up with the world's appetite.

Junk food satisfies briefly, followed by long periods of guilt and sorrow. We hold up the empty bag of chips and say, "What have I done?" We wake up with a hangover and mutter for mercy.

Junk food masks itself as food we need. Take, for example, sex before marriage. It looks like love on the packaging, but inside it's junk food, stuffed with regret and dissatisfaction.

When we love someone with God's love, there is no regret or hunger pains two minutes or two weeks later. Why? Because God fills and satisfies us. His promises bring eternal fulfillment, not temporary appeasement.

We work to feed our appetites;
Meanwhile our souls go hungry.
ECCLESIASTES 6:7, *THE MESSAGE*

The Israelites turned to a golden calf—a fast-food, Golden Arches cow—over the USDA-Approved, prime-choice God. They ate fast food served by obscene gods to meet their immediate need, and then they learned their lesson.

Instead of looking up to Mount Sinai where God literally was, they looked down at their camp to find a god to worship. They paid for their mistake for years to come. If they had only "held up" to God their intentions of building a golden calf, to check it all out, they would have gotten a look of disapproval and tossed it aside, saving time and many lives.

Our draw to junk food never satisfies. We think it's good for us now, but later, when we step on the scales, we know we made a mistake. We feel terrible. We look terrible.

Sin also feels good at the time, but when it's over, we hate ourselves and feel terrible.

However, God's food always offers us something better to look up to.

Health Food

When Jesus chose the food to serve at the Feeding of the Fish Sandwiches, he chose something healthy—no raisin pastries, chocolate-covered figs, or double-battered fried fish sticks—but whole grain bread and fresh fish.

Today's doctors wearing white lab coats and carrying clipboards would have nodded approvingly as they stood by Jesus, watching the pounds of bread and fish pass by.

Breads, especially made from whole grains like those found in the first century, provide fiber to your diet, promoting digestive health and even helping your heart.

> A diet high in whole grain foods is associated with a significantly lower risk of developing cardiovascular disease, including heart disease and stroke. . . .
>
> A grain is "whole" when the entire grain seed is retained: the bran, germ and the endosperm. The bran and germ components are rich in fiber, vitamins, minerals, antioxidants, and healthy fats. These are the parts removed in the refining process, leaving behind the energy-dense but nutrient-poor endosperm portion of the grain. . . .
>
> [Philip Mellen, MD, said,] "Greater whole grain intake is associated with less obesity, diabetes, high blood pressure, and high cholesterol—major factors that increase the risk for heart disease and stroke."[3]

The refining process removes the "whole" grain and offers a weak substitute, still calling it "whole." Don't be fooled by this refinement. Check the fine print.[4]

Fish provides our bodies with two polyunsaturated oils, omega-3 and omega-6, both good for our hearts, our brains, and even—some studies say—our vision.

> Continuing research involves the role of omega-3 fatty acids and the immune system, and suggests a positive influence on rheumatoid arthritis, asthma, lupus, kidney disease and cancer, as well as promising research at the National Institutes of Health on depression.[5]

Two of the most important nutrients are flaxseed and fish oil, helpful for the heart, circulation, and reducing cholesterol. Flaxseed oil comes from a grain or seed. Fish oil comes from, well, a fish.

Grains and fish . . . both good for the heart. Even our pharmacists know that.

So does the Bible. These two menu items appear over and over again in its pages:

- Unleavened bread at Passover[6] symbolized God's powerful salvation of the Israelites.
- Manna from heaven fed the Israelites[7] and taught them a healthy lesson about faith in God.
- Jonah, himself in an unhealthy place, was swallowed by a big fish, who taught Jonah a valuable lesson, then spit him in the right direction.[8]
- Jesus came from a healthy lineage in Bethlehem, which means "house of bread."[9]
- Jesus picked fishermen to spread the Good News[10] for spiritual health.

- Jesus used bread at the Passover meal to symbolize that his broken body would restore us to a healthy relationship with God.[11]
- Jesus performed miracles with fish (the huge catch following a night of bad fishing,[12] the tax coin in the fish's mouth[13]) to show his strength and power.
- Jesus called himself "the bread of life."[14]

Bread and fish have become God's symbols for spiritual health in the Bible. No wonder they were the only menu items at the fish-sandwich buffet. When Jesus looked up, he knew he had received God's Grade-A stamp of approval.

When I eat out, I always look for that one section of the menu called "Healthy Choices" or "Lite Fare" or "For Those Who Think They Are Fat." It's usually on the back, stuffed in the bottom corner. It's there. You just have to look for it.

GOD KNOWS OUR SPIRITS. IT'S HIS WILL THAT WE REMAIN SPIRITUALLY HEALTHY.

Since God made our bodies, he knows how we can live physically healthy. He designed our bodies to eat the right foods—foods like fish and bread. It's his will that we eat healthily.

Likewise, God knows our spirits. It's also his will that we remain spiritually healthy. He knows how to feed our souls with sinless choices. We must pass by the world's unhealthy menu items and find those things that offer us the best diet for spiritual health.

God's Diet Plan

Any diet plan can succeed if we do three things:

1. Read the instructions—know the parameters and limitations of the diet;
2. Obey the coach—do what the plan says; and
3. Stick to the plan—commit and remain steadfast.

Following God's will for our lives is like going on a diet. To receive the benefits of God's diet plan—his will for our lives— we have to look up and keep our focus on him. We must make good choices and say *no* to bad ones. He promises us healthy, more productive lives if only we follow a few basic steps:

These commandments that I give you today are to be on your hearts. Impress them on your children. Talk about them when you sit at home and when you walk along the road, when you lie down and when you get up. Tie them as symbols on your hands and bind them on your foreheads. Write them on the doorframes of your houses and on your gates.

DEUTERONOMY 6:6-9

Read the Instructions

Moses told us to put reminders of the spiritual-diet plan all over our houses. In fact, he said to write it on our foreheads and the backs of our hands just in case we forget. The Bible must also be consumed into our hearts and allowed to filter into every inch of our lives.

God told the prophet Ezekiel to do this literally:

He said to me, "Son of man, eat what is before you, eat this scroll; then go and speak to the people of Israel." So I opened my mouth, and he gave me the scroll to eat.

Then he said to me, "Son of man, eat this scroll I am giving you and fill your stomach with it." So I ate it, and it tasted as sweet as honey in my mouth.

EZEKIEL 3:1-3

Please don't try this at home! You don't have to sit down at dinnertime and eat the pages of the Minor Prophets. To us, this is a metaphor for ingesting God's Word deep into ourselves. So read the Word. Hear the Word. Make the Word part of your daily schedule. Dine on it regularly.

There's a series of books out called Eat This, Not That! They offer healthy alternatives to unhealthy foods, showing pictures of the bad stuff and directing you to the good.

In a way, it's like the Bible: Do This, Not That! The Bible shows us sin and then says, *Do this instead.* Jesus taught this in the Sermon on the Mount:

You have heard that it was said, "Eye for eye, and tooth for tooth." But I tell you, do not resist an evil person. If anyone slaps you on the right cheek, turn to them the other cheek also.

MATTHEW 5:38-39

You have heard that it was said, "Love your neighbor and hate your enemy." But I tell you, love your enemies and pray for those who persecute you.

MATTHEW 5:43-44

Do grace, not retaliation.
Do love, not hate.

Once you become so familiar with God's will, you can spot junk food a mile away.

Obey the Coach

Body coaches demand obedience. They scream in their students' ears. They curse at them when they fail. They make them do difficult, painful things. Why?

Body coaches want their students to lose weight and be healthy. It's what the students want. That's why they're paying the big bucks!

DO GRACE, NOT RETALIATION. DO LOVE, NOT HATE.

Yet when God calls for obedience, he gets a bad reputation.

"God seems to be mad all the time."

"God's no fun; he makes me do things I don't want to do."

"God has impossible rules."

The Israelites in the desert were fired up about God when they arrived at Mount Sinai. They were ready to stick to the plan.

> The people all responded together, "We will do everything the LORD has said."
> EXODUS 19:8

God rolled out the laws and rules—four chapters full. The people loved it.

> When Moses went and told the people all the LORD's words and laws, they responded with one voice, "Everything the LORD has said we will do."
> EXODUS 24:3

Moses disappeared up the mountain with God to get more instructions. He was gone for forty days, and in the meantime, the people scrapped the plan and created their own.

> When the people saw that Moses was so long in coming
> down from the mountain, they gathered around Aaron
> and said, "Come, make us gods who will go before
> us. As for this fellow Moses who brought us up out of
> Egypt, we don't know what has happened to him."
> EXODUS 32:1

Wow—before even forty days had passed, they were done. Doesn't seem very long.

Most people give up their New Year's resolutions within a month, and only about 8 percent can stick it out for an entire year.[15] Researchers found that if you do something healthy on a regular basis, it takes an average of sixty-six days before it becomes cemented into your mind as a routine habit.[16] If only the Israelites had lasted another twenty-six days, they would have been okay.

God wants spiritual health for us, too, which requires shedding those worldly pleasures from our lives and living sinlessly slim and trim. He knows the plan is hard, and he's doing everything he can to motivate us down the right path. God demands total obedience to his will to get us where we need to go.

As you read the Word, listen to God's commands and purpose to exercise them in your life.

> Jesus replied, "Anyone who loves me will obey my
> teaching. My Father will love them, and we will come
> to them and make our home with them. Anyone who

does not love me will not obey my teaching. These words you hear are not my own; they belong to the Father who sent me."
JOHN 14:23-24

We are meant not only to hear and know but also to listen and do. Obedience is not *knowing* what you are supposed to do. Obedience is *doing* what you are supposed to do.

> Stay away from sin.
> Embrace God's commands.

OBEDIENCE IS NOT KNOWING *WHAT YOU ARE SUPPOSED TO DO*. OBEDIENCE IS DOING *WHAT YOU ARE SUPPOSED TO DO*.

Stick to the Plan

A diet only works if you stick with it for the rest of your life. To do so, you must commit to the diet with everything inside you.

Love the LORD your God with all your heart and with all your soul and with all your strength.
DEUTERONOMY 6:5

In 2010, my wife and I chose to become vegetarians, cutting meat (and some dairy) out of our diets. Frustrated with our weight, our cholesterol levels, and the medications we were taking (Barbie experienced side effects from post-breast-cancer meds), we made a tremendous decision that changed everything. We said good-bye to foods we love.

Since then, I've also reduced the amount of coffee and sodium in my diet because of high blood pressure. Is there anything left to eat?

However, we cannot deny the results: Better health. Better sense of well-being. No medications. We didn't make this change for the time being—we made this choice for forever. It was hard, but it was worth it.

If we stick to God's healthy menu of choices for the rest of our lives, we will begin to see positive effects in our relationships, fulfillment in our hearts, and a closer walk with the one who designed the plan in the first place.

The Promise of Spiritual Health

Sin is the world's junk food. If I work to feed my appetite with the menu items of this world, my soul starves to death.

If I turn to God and dine off his diet plan, I receive the exact ingredients needed to survive in a sinful world.

> Let them give thanks to the LORD for his unfailing love
> and his wonderful deeds for mankind,
> for he satisfies the thirsty
> and fills the hungry with good things.
> PSALM 107:8-9

God's diet plan consists of the whole-grain promises of God's power, God's ability, and God's love. He has the strength to save us from our troubles, lead us in the right direction, give us wonderful blessings, and satisfy our thirst and hunger. These truths should make up our daily diets.

When we forget them, we get overwhelmed, burdened, bloated, weighed down.

The Feeding of the Fish Sandwiches shows that God does not promise us junk. What he promises is healthy for us, and it can't be found in the world. Sin looks good, tastes good, and usually costs less at the checkout, but it costs more in the long run, making us fat and bloated with unnecessary regret and guilt.

So put down the Doritos of sin and follow God.

Dine on his plan of purity—promising spiritual nutrition for your soul and your heart.

Read the labels found in his Word.

Keep looking up for guidance and approval from God, and stop looking down at the world for relief.

If you do, things will begin looking up.

Saying Grace

Lord, your will for me is simple and healthy: Stay away from sin. So keep me away from temptation and save me from the tempter. I do not want to get fat on the unnecessary weight of the world. I desire a lean life, lived purely for you, just as you promised. God, refresh my soul, fill my body, and revive my heart.

He put you through hard times. He made
you go hungry. Then he fed you with manna,
something neither you nor your parents knew
anything about, so you would learn that men
and women don't live by bread only; we live by
every word that comes from GOD's mouth.

DEUTERONOMY 8:3, *THE MESSAGE*

#7

MIRACLE

The Promise of God's Power

Taking the five loaves and the two fish and looking up to heaven, he
gave thanks and broke the loaves. Then he gave them to his disciples to
distribute to the people. He also divided the two fish among them all.

MARK 6:41

THE 1980 US Men's Olympic Hockey Team, made up of amateurs and an untested coach, was not expected to go very far. And due to Russia's invasion of Afghanistan, political tensions were high. The legendary Russian hockey team almost boycotted the Winter Games since President Jimmy Carter was considering a boycott of the Summer Games to be held in Moscow later that year. But despite these factors, the US team surprised everyone.[1]

Coming back from an exhibition loss to Russia, the Americans defeated such powerhouse teams as Czechoslovakia and Sweden to arrive at the finals, once again meeting their on-and-off-the-ice archrivals, the Russians. In a close and exciting game watched by millions of Americans, the US beat Russia 4–3. ABC commentator Al Michaels delivered this memorable line at the very end:

Eleven seconds . . . you've got ten seconds, the countdown
going on right now, Morrow up to Silk, five seconds left
in the game. Do you believe in miracles? *Yes!*[2]

The game has since been known as the "Miracle on Ice." A
movie starring Kurt Russell as Coach Herb Brooks used that
term—*Miracle*—for its title.

But was it really a miracle?

Sure, the odds were against the Americans, who had not
always been particularly strong at hockey. They didn't have a
lot of experience, but Herb Brooks's style of coaching was discipline, hard work, and 100 percent effort. The Russians made
some critical errors during the game that were costly.

But does a win by the US constitute a miracle? Did the
puck magically take left and right turns during game play? Did
players lift off the ground and hover over the ice? Did a player
smacked dead by a wayward puck suddenly get up and return
to the game?

Hardly. The US won because of coaching, discipline, hard
work, 100 percent effort, mistakes by the other team, and per-
haps a bit of luck.

Our world's definition of a miracle is simply anything that is
incredible or unbelievable. You could call your computer manufacturer with a technical question, get through to an operator
without waiting on hold, and have your problem solved in less
than one minute. Miracle? You could try to get a seat on a plane,
find out it's sold out in coach, and receive a free upgrade to first
class. Miracle? You could find a parking place at the mall, right
up front, the day after Thanksgiving. Miracle?

While as impressive and amazing as some moments may be,
we cannot call these incidents miracles in the truest, biblical sense.

The fish-sandwich events are two of the most widespread miracles Jesus performed: They affected thousands, not just one or two people. The ability to create so much food transcended anything ever imagined possible.

How did Jesus do this miracle? We don't know, and we shouldn't know, because once we think we know, it'll cease to be a miracle.

Bread and fish appeared out of nowhere and were delivered to the starving people.

So while we look at the promises of God as revealed through the fish-sandwich events, it brings up the question—are miracles promised by God today? Can we expect miracles when we need them? Will amazing abundance suddenly rain down on our lives?

Miracles

Miracles in the Bible are exhibitions of God's power altering the natural occurrences on earth. God performed a number of miracles in the Old Testament:

- Creation—causing something to come from nothing[3]
- The Red Sea—parting a body of water so a few million people could walk through it[4]
- Manna/quail/water—providing water and food to the Israelites in the desert for forty years, with manna and quail that came out of nowhere[5]
- The Jordan River—parting a flowing river so millions could walk through it[6]
- Jericho—toppling the walls of a city with trumpet blasts and shouts[7]
- Joshua—causing the sun to stand still during a battle with the Amorites[8]

Jesus followed those up with his miracles in the New Testament:

- Water to wine—turning H_2O into fermented grape juice[9]
- Taxes—causing money to appear in a fish's mouth so Jesus could pay the Temple tax[10]
- Leprosy—reversing the effects of the crippling disease[11]
- Blindness—helping the blind to see[12]
- Demoniac—causing an insane man to become sane[13]
- Death—raising Lazarus and a little girl from the dead[14]
- Walking on water—taking a shortcut over the Sea of Galilee during a storm[15]
- Transfiguration—appearing in his glorious form with Moses and Elijah by his side[16]
- Resurrection—bringing himself back to life after a brutal crucifixion[17]

These are miracles—they defy all natural explanation and occurred right in front of eyewitnesses. The Feedings of the Five Thousand and Four Thousand fit right in that category. If there were fifteen thousand people—counting the men, women, and children—present at this one time at the Feeding of the Five Thousand, and, let's say, everyone got one fish and one loaf of bread (a pretty satisfying meal), then that means Jesus caused more than fifteen thousand cooked fish and fifteen thousand baked loaves of bread to appear out of nowhere. Add the numbers for the Feeding of the Four Thousand (that's twelve thousand with men, women, and children), and now you're talking twenty-seven thousand cooked fish and twenty-seven thousand loaves of baked bread between the two miracles.

The disciples saw it with their own eyes.

The people ate it with their own mouths.

The incredible numbers exceeded any human, pre–Industrial Revolution, mass food-production explanation.

That's a miracle!

Today, however, we wonder . . . *Where is that power today?* We pray for money, and it doesn't appear in our pockets. We pray for our sick, and they don't suddenly get better. We plead for peace and see nothing but war. Will we ever see a miraculous fish sandwich in our lifetime?

Let's look at why miracles occurred in the Bible.

God's Identity

Changes in airport security have inconvenienced all of us. One of the most aggravating things for me is showing my ID to every person I pass: The curbside service. The check-in person. The baggage screener. The person before walking through X-ray. The person after walking through X-ray. The security person at the gate. The flight attendant. The captain. The copilot. The airport bathroom janitor and his assistant. How many times do I have to prove to everyone that I am who I say I am?

God is asked all the time to prove himself, and yet, when the proofs of his identity are shown, it's never good enough.

God introduced himself to the Israelites in the Old Testament through miracles. Jesus introduced himself to the Israelites in the New Testament through miracles. He mirrored the miracles of the Old Testament so people would draw the lines of conclusion.

Jesus wasn't the first to feed multiple people in the Bible.

Recall Exodus 16, where the Israelites had just escaped from the Egyptians at the Red Sea. Immediately their stomachs grumbled, causing them to grumble.

"We're hungry!"

Moses turned to God for help. God fed them miraculously by raining down a type of pasty honey bread every morning.

> The LORD said to Moses, "I will rain down bread from heaven for you. The people are to go out each day and gather enough for that day. In this way I will test them and see whether they will follow my instructions." . . .
> The people of Israel called the bread manna. It was white like coriander seed and tasted like wafers made with honey.
> EXODUS 16:4, 31

In 1 Kings 17, Elijah made his dramatic debut, calling for a stoppage of rain during the reign of Ahab, which caused a famine. The Lord directed him to a town where a widow would feed him. When he arrived, he saw a widow and asked her for some bread.

> "As surely as the LORD your God lives," she replied, "I don't have any bread—only a handful of flour in a jar and a little olive oil in a jug. I am gathering a few sticks to take home and make a meal for myself and my son, that we may eat it—and die."
> Elijah said to her, "Don't be afraid. Go home and do as you have said. But first make a small loaf of bread for me from what you have and bring it to me, and then make something for yourself and your son. For this is what the LORD, the God of Israel, says: 'The jar of flour will not be used up and the jug of oil will not run dry until the day the LORD sends rain on the land.'"

She went away and did as Elijah had told her. So there was food every day for Elijah and for the woman and her family. For the jar of flour was not used up and the jug of oil did not run dry, in keeping with the word of the LORD spoken by Elijah.

1 KINGS 17:12-16

In a land of drought, God caused a miraculous multiplication of the ingredients that make bread—flour and oil.

Then came another man of God, Elisha.

A man came from Baal Shalishah, bringing the man of God twenty loaves of barley bread baked from the first ripe grain, along with some heads of new grain. "Give it to the people to eat," Elisha said.

"How can I set this before a hundred men?" his servant asked.

But Elisha answered, "Give it to the people to eat. For this is what the LORD says: 'They will eat and have some left over.'" Then he set it before them, and they ate and had some left over, according to the word of the LORD.

2 KINGS 4:42-44

So did Jesus plagiarize their miracles on purpose?

Yes.

Through Moses, God fed millions of people bread thousands of times for forty years. Elijah fed three people hundreds of times over the years. Elisha fed a hundred at one time.

Jesus fed thousands of people fully baked bread twice and, not to be outdone, threw in cooked fish, too. Jesus confirmed to the people that he could do the bread thing that the prophets did, only better. He was more than a prophet.

Maybe at the Transfiguration, God wanted to showcase Jesus' ID by adding him to the Bread Makers Hall of Fame—Moses, Elijah, Elisha,[18] and Jesus, with Jesus at the center as the chief baker.

Word definitely spread about Jesus because of the miracles. He got the attention of the people because of his "signs":

> Now there was a Pharisee, a man named Nicodemus who
> was a member of the Jewish ruling council. He came to
> Jesus at night and said, "Rabbi, we know that you are
> a teacher who has come from God. For no one could
> perform the signs you are doing if God were not with
> him."
>
> JOHN 3:1-2

> Still, many in the crowd believed in him. They said,
> "When the Messiah comes, will he perform more signs
> than this man?"
>
> JOHN 7:31

The Pharisees clearly acknowledged Jesus' miracles and knew something was up with this guy. They saw his ID but didn't believe it.

That ability to perform miracles was passed on to his disciples, who spread the gospel to a wider area. Once again, they carried the proof that their message was true by means of the miraculous.

So, does Jesus have to do miracles today to prove that he is God? Jesus sufficiently introduced himself and showed his qualifications as God to the world. He doesn't need to show his identification any longer. His ID became the Bible. His past miracles still qualify him as God today.

Jesus' ID does not expire like my driver's license. My photo ID indicates how much I've changed over the years. Jesus does not change. Who he was in the past is who he is today.

If Jesus did miracles in the past, he can still do miracles today. But if people saw miracles today, would they believe?

Jesus told a story about a humble believer named Lazarus,[19] who died and went to heaven, where he was comforted by Abraham himself, and a proud rich man who died and went to hell, a place of torture and pain. The gap between heaven and hell opened, and the rich man asked Abraham if Lazarus could cool his tongue with water.[20] Abraham denied the request. So . . .

> He [the rich man] answered, "Then I beg you, father, send Lazarus to my family, for I have five brothers. Let him warn them, so that they will not also come to this place of torment."
>
> Abraham replied, "They have Moses and the Prophets; let them listen to them."
>
> "No, father Abraham," he said, "but if someone from the dead goes to them, they will repent."
>
> He said to him, "If they do not listen to Moses and the Prophets, they will not be convinced even if someone rises from the dead."
>
> LUKE 16:27-31

The rich man asked for a display of God's power, something miraculous, to wake up his doomed brothers. Abraham told him they had the written text of the Scriptures, a historical biography of God's ID. A miracle wouldn't make any difference up against such stubborn hearts.

The brothers weren't the only ones who had a hard time believing:

> Even after Jesus had performed so many signs in their
> presence, they still would not believe in him.
> JOHN 12:37

Really? Right in front of their eyes, and no response? What happened? Aren't miracles what everyone needs to believe? People demanded more proof from Jesus all the time. Jesus rebuffed them.

> Some of the Pharisees and teachers of the law said to
> him, "Teacher, we want to see a sign from you."
> He answered, "A wicked and adulterous generation
> asks for a sign! But none will be given it except the sign of
> the prophet Jonah. For as Jonah was three days and three
> nights in the belly of a huge fish, so the Son of Man will
> be three days and three nights in the heart of the earth."
> MATTHEW 12:38-40

Demanding more proof from God offends him, just like how I feel when twelve people demand to see my ID at the airport. To answer the Pharisees' request, Jesus said, "If you want to see the miraculous, check out the story of Jonah." Then he tells them, "I'll also do something pretty incredible soon, when I rise from the dead." No additional evidence was needed. Look to the Bible and Jesus' resurrection for all the miracles you need in order to believe.

It doesn't mean God can't or won't do miracles. It's just that he's already proven himself.

Miracle Baskets

When my brother-in-law Neils dispensed his theory on the Feeding of the Five Thousand, I thought he was joking. At the time, he was not my brother-in-law, but a new staff member at church who taught a men's Bible study. I signed up since I was new to this whole Christian thing and wanted to bounce some questions off someone.

He said, "Some believe the Feedings of the Five Thousand and Four Thousand were nothing more than big ol' potlucks."

An unsettling spirit entered the room. *Say what?*

He continued. "C'mon, no Israelite at that time would ever hit the road without packing a supper. What Jesus was able to do was encourage everyone to share what they had on them with those around them."

Neils always loved to twist the screws to make us question, defend, and then believe, but he didn't make up this theory. Many have pushed this idea of the world's first church potluck to take the miraculous out of the miracle, just as the Resurrection has come under attack with its own share of outlandish theories.

So were the fish-sandwich feedings amazing displays of community caring and sharing? The sharing theory with the Feeding of the Five Thousand just doesn't add up for a number of reasons:

1. Jesus actually suggested a potluck by telling the disciples to gather up all the food they could find. No luck. Only a boy with five loaves and two fish had any food.

2. Mark 6:41 reads, "He also divided the two fish among them all." This means that five thousand people ate from two fish. This doesn't say five thousand people divided up two fish into teeny, tiny bites, nor does it say five thousand people followed Jesus' example of sharing his fish and likewise shared with those around them.

3. Right after the account of the Feeding of the Five Thousand, John 6:14 reads, "After the people saw the sign Jesus performed, they began to say, 'Surely this is the Prophet who is to come into the world.'" What is so miraculous about getting people to share? I did this all the time with my boys when they were young. "Give your brother a grape!" Hardly a miracle . . . though, some days . . .

4. John 6:14-15 states that the people had two ideas about Jesus after this: They considered him a prophet, and they wanted to make him a king. "This man convinces people to share. He must be a man of God! With power like this, he'll defeat the mighty Romans!" You can taste my sarcasm here.

5. In John 6:41-59, Jesus compared himself with the manna from heaven that fed the Israelites in the desert. The manna, everyone agreed, was a miraculous incident. Would Jesus do any less when he was trying to convince the religious leaders—and avid Moses lovers—that he was greater than Moses by doing a substandard miracle?

One of the reasons people give for the potluck theory is that the presence of baskets at the miracle supposedly proves that people brought a picnic to the event. That's a weak argument, because Jesus usually arrived in towns unannounced. There weren't Groupon and direct-marketing options to advertise his appearance. Someone probably yelled in the city square, "Hey, that guy Jesus is here!"—which was probably followed by a mad scramble to find him.

No time to cook some fish and bake some bread. You would run as fast as you could to find him before he left. People were probably on their way to the market, carrying their "shopping carts," when they slipped into the huge revival held by Jesus. Maybe any food they had with them had been eaten hours previously. Remember, Jesus said these people had been with him for days. Certainly, the disciples would have run to people carrying baskets of fish and asked them to donate their food to the potluck. So nobody had anything to eat; those baskets were void of food. Where did the baskets come from that Jesus filled at the end of the miracle?

As the food multiplication occurred, maybe the people donated their empty baskets to the cause. Out of fifteen thousand, it seems likely that at least twelve people had baskets on them.

But let's just imagine something for a second. What if nobody brought baskets to the meeting with Jesus? There's no indication in the Gospel accounts of anyone bringing a basket to the event. What if God made the baskets right there, right then, on the spot? Can't a God who has the power to make bread and fish appear out of nowhere miraculously weave some baskets to hold it all in?

We never refer to this as the miracle of fish, bread, and baskets, but maybe it is. Maybe Jesus made baskets, too. Is that overly difficult to fathom?

If we admit the unlimited power of Jesus to multiply fish sandwiches, why limit him when it comes to other matters . . .

like baskets? You think catching fish takes a long time? Try making a basket in a millisecond!

Why are the baskets important to stop and consider?

As stated earlier in the chapter, God isn't required to do miracles to prove himself to the world, but he still has the power to do whatever he wants, whenever he wants, in any way he wants, whether before our eyes or behind the scenes. We have to believe that. If people need baskets, Jesus can provide.

If we live thinking God is no longer in the miracle business, we've limited his power and his love for us.

It's the potential of that power appearing in unexpected ways that gives us power during our weakest times, knowing that at any moment, God could miraculously cause a woven basket to appear on our doorsteps. He could possibly do the impossible.

His baskets can be full of food or used to carry us when we're down. His baskets show the amazingly woven intricacies of our lives, as God weaves people and opportunities onto our paths. His baskets are stuffed with his loving-kindness and grace.

The idea of the miracle baskets tells me that God could work behind the scenes in unpredictable, unplanned, and unlimited ways—ways many probably will not notice.

We don't know that Jesus multiplied baskets, but we must believe that he can.

If you limit him, you don't know him.

The Promise of Power

I love it when I see people for the first time in years and they say, "You look the same." When you get older, that thought brings a smile to your face.

When I went to my twentieth high-school reunion, a woman

there said, "Everyone else here is losing their hair. You're the only one who has gained hair." I tossed back my long mane, stroked my groomed goatee, and laughed. Being six foot six has its advantages. Nobody can see the ever-widening bald spot on the top of my head.

IF YOU LIMIT JESUS, YOU DON'T KNOW HIM.

God never changes. He, too, always looks the same. At every reunion, he hears that.

> Jesus Christ is the same yesterday and today and forever.
> HEBREWS 13:8

There are two explanations for whether God does miracles today as he did in biblical times:

Option #1—God did lots of miracles at a very special time in biblical history, then stopped. The frequency of miracles ran red hot during the time of Jesus and the apostles, which lasted a limited time, but now God chooses not to do miracles; he must figure he did everything he needed to prove himself.

Option #2—God does miracles today just as in biblical times; we just don't hear about them, see them, or attribute them to him.

Option #1 describes a God who can do miracles but won't. He sees hurt and pain, then shrugs, saying, "Oh well, they had their chance" or "Oh well, someday they'll be in heaven and all their troubles will be far away." This is a cold, uncaring, insensitive picture of a loving God.

Option #2 makes more sense. If Jesus Christ could perform

miracles two thousand years ago, he still can today. His heart broke for those hurting then, so it still does now. His desire to heal never changes. He's the same yesterday, today, and tomorrow.

The second option describes a compassionate God who wants to get involved even though he doesn't have to. Yes, he's proven himself, but he can't help loving us and refuses to sit back and do nothing.

Who's to say that God hasn't done something miraculous in the life of every one of the seven-plus billion people on this planet, at some time, through someone, with something no one can explain? Maybe he's even doing it right now.

It all depends on how you define a miracle.

While in Costa Rica on a mission trip, a few of us visited the home of a woman who took dozens of pills every day for a number of aches and ailments. We prayed for her in English and Spanish. When we finished, the woman was trembling. She felt healed. The pain had subsided. That night at a meeting, she brought all her pills, threw them to the ground, and declared God had healed her. Her husband, a non-Christian, couldn't believe his eyes. Miracle?

In 2010, Nadia Bloom got lost in a thick, swampy forest near her home in Winter Springs, Florida. After days of searching, crews were giving up hope. A member of her church, James King, felt God telling him to walk in the direction of the sunrise. He did and discovered Nadia alive deep in the woods, among the brush.[21] Nobody could believe his story, especially the media. Police grilled James, and no guilt was discovered. Miracle?

I've known too many people who'd learned they had cancer or a tumor, only to show up for a scan or surgery and be told "It's not there" by a board-certified medical doctor.

Based on my experience and scores of claims from firsthand

witnesses, I would say miracles do exist today. The media often calls them coincidences, realizations, or chance, but we know better.

To say there are no miracles is to say God has lost his power or is not involved with his creation. Neither statement can be true. God has a hands-on policy when it comes to the world today, and he manifests his power in our lives because he loves us. He just doesn't have to do those miracles to the degree he did before, when he needed to reveal his true nature and purpose.

I love how the Gospel of John ends:

> Jesus performed many other signs in the presence of his disciples, which are not recorded in this book. But these are written that you may believe that Jesus is the Messiah, the Son of God, and that by believing you may have life in his name.
>
> JOHN 20:30-31

Don't you wonder what those other miracles were that weren't miraculous enough to make it into the four Gospels? Maybe they were low-key, quiet displays of his power that didn't attract a lot of media attention, but they were special enough to still be called miracles—much the same way God operates today.

GOD HAS A HANDS-ON POLICY WHEN IT COMES TO THE WORLD TODAY.

Remember, a miracle is any time God steps in and redirects the natural occurrences of life. Big or small.

He still inspires a heart. He whispers an idea. He changes the wind direction. He influences the stock market. He stops traffic.

God's power has never changed. The God who made

thousands of miraculous fish sandwiches has the same power to work in new, quiet, and unexpected ways in your life today.

Don't expect them. Don't demand them. Look for them.

Know that if God wants to miraculously make you a sandwich or weave a basket or find you a job or cure your illness or find your prodigal son or fix your marriage, he can.

Saying Grace

Lord, thank you for the power you send into my life. Thank you for working in ways that I don't always see. Thank you for showing yourself and your miraculous hand in the circumstances and people in my life. I know you have the power to do all things according to your will. You know the areas in my life where I need that power right now. I'm comforted knowing you can multiply, deliver, and weave yourself into any situation.

Now he who supplies seed to the sower and bread for food will also supply and increase your store of seed and will enlarge the harvest of your righteousness. You will be enriched in every way so that you can be generous on every occasion, and through us your generosity will result in thanksgiving to God.

2 CORINTHIANS 9:10-11

GROUPS OF FIFTY

The Promise of Community

*Another of his disciples, Andrew, Simon Peter's brother, spoke
up, "Here is a boy with five small barley loaves and two
small fish, but how far will they go among so many?"*

JOHN 6:8-9

*He said to his disciples, "Have them sit down in groups of about fifty each."
The disciples did so, and everyone sat down. Taking the five loaves
and the two fish and looking up to heaven, he gave thanks and broke
them. Then he gave them to the disciples to distribute to the people.*

LUKE 9:14-16

EVER SINCE I was in middle school, I've dreamed of winning an
Academy Award for Best Original Screenplay. I have watched the
Academy Awards in their entirety, never taking my eyes off the
screen except for biological necessity, tossing in my guesses for
Best Picture, Best Actor, Best Actress, even Best Film and Sound
Editing, although I have no clue how they judge for that kind
of stuff. Afterward, I find myself rehearsing my own acceptance
speech for weeks.

Probably the hardest part of the speech begins with these four
words: "I'd like to thank . . ." That's when the pressure sets in.

Whom do I thank and in what order? The director . . . the stars . . . the producer . . . the production assistant who brought me water . . . my agent . . . my publicist . . . craft service . . .

How can I forget all the people who helped me find my love for the entertainment business? Miss Freize, my English teacher from seventh grade, who encouraged my love of writing . . . Mr. Haider, my film production teacher from high school, who gave us bratty kids a camera and the opportunity to make films . . . my dad, who took me to work at KYW-TV in Philadelphia and showed me how the business works . . . my friends Ned and Jeff, who read my scripts and gave me feedback . . .

How about family . . . my wife . . . my kids . . . who put up with my dream through good and bad, poverty and wealth?

Can I thank all of them in one minute before the band plays me offstage?

Then again, another side of me wants to shortcut the entire process and just scream out, "I'd like to thank . . . ME! I did it all! I'm the one being honored here! Clap for me! Bow to me! (Insert diabolical laugh.)"

That would never work. It didn't for *Titanic*'s James Cameron, who stood up to accept the award for Best Director and shouted the line from the movie, "I'm the king of the world!" It came off as arrogant and self-important.

The truth is, I could not have gotten where I am today without the help of others.

One of the most overlooked aspects of the mass feedings is that as Jesus produced the miraculous abundance of food, he told the disciples to organize the people into groups of fifty. He used a community to complete the miracle. God brought others into the process to kick-start it, distribute it, and maintain it. Without others, the fish sandwiches would have rotted and spoiled in a big pile at Jesus' feet.

Our need for others goes all the way back to Creation. God looked at the first created man, Adam, and said it wasn't good for him to be alone.[1] We need the help and support of a community, so God promises to draw other people into our lives—bringing with them their talents, gifts, and strengths—when we need them most.

During the Feeding of the Fish Sandwiches, Jesus used the talents of advisers, givers, and servers, just like he does today.

Advisers

When Jesus began both feedings, he did something interesting. He asked the disciples what he should do. Really? Jesus asked his friends for advice?

- *The five thousand*: "When Jesus looked up and saw a great crowd coming toward him, he said to Philip, 'Where shall we buy bread for these people to eat?' He asked this only to test him, for he already had in mind what he was going to do." (John 6:5-6)

- *The four thousand*: "During those days another large crowd gathered. Since they had nothing to eat, Jesus called his disciples to him and said, 'I have compassion for these people; they have already been with me three days and have nothing to eat. If I send them home hungry, they will collapse on the way, because some of them have come a long distance.'" (Mark 8:1-3)

Both times, the disciples responded in similar fashion:

- *The five thousand*: "Philip answered him, 'It would take more than half a year's wages to buy enough bread for each one to have a bite!'" (John 6:7)

- *The four thousand*: "His disciples answered, 'But where in this remote place can anyone get enough bread to feed them?'" (Mark 8:4)

So why did Jesus probe the disciples for advice? Scripture either says he already knew what he was going to do or implies that Jesus was quite aware they were nowhere near a marketplace. Why did Jesus ask for an idea when he already knew what he was going to do?

It's possible . . .

- Jesus knew they were going to suggest the boy's supper idea.
- Philip coincidentally had the same idea that Jesus was thinking.
- Jesus had a totally different idea, ditched it, and decided to use this new suggestion to make the disciples feel like a part of the process. This doesn't mean his original idea was wrong, but to involve the disciples, Jesus used their idea.

Or maybe Jesus asked the disciples the same way I used to ask my kids for their advice when I already knew the answer:

- "When do you think we should do our chores?"
- "Why do you think homework is important?"
- "How do you think you should be punished?"

During these times, I really wanted my kids to be thinking about their own situations. I wanted to hear what they had to say and make them a part of the final decision. If not, they became too reliant on me as the authority figure to make all the decisions. I'm not going to be around forever. Jesus probably addressed his followers the same way. "What do you think we should do? You know, I'm not going to be around here forever."

Maybe Jesus is interested in our ideas. We have brains; God knows that . . . He made them. He wants us to use them. A mind is a terrible thing to waste, as the saying goes. Jesus didn't roll his eyes or dismiss the disciples' plan. He seemed open to their ideas and used what they suggested.

We are created in God's image. We reveal his qualities in our compassion, creativity, and brainstorming. We have the capacity to think like God, if only we try.

But our knowledge is limited. We do not have all the answers. So God wants us to brainstorm with others—a community think tank.

Plans fail for lack of counsel,
    but with many advisers they succeed.
PROVERBS 15:22

It's godly to obtain advice. Even the wisest man in the Bible—King Solomon, who wrote the proverb above—realized he needed the best advisers.

When we face financial, relational, or career problems, God places people in our paths to help us figure out our next steps and give us the answers we need.

I remember when our pastor approached me to work on staff at a time when I needed direction.

I remember facing financial strain, wondering what we were going to do next, when a producer called and asked if I wanted to work on a children's animated series.

WE HAVE THE CAPACITY TO THINK LIKE GOD, IF ONLY WE TRY. BUT OUR KNOWLEDGE IS LIMITED.

I remember once, during a period when I was speaking on finding joy in prison, using Philippians as my platform, I met a prison guard while I was writing a message. Believe me, I don't hang out with prison guards, so this was amazing, and his insight was tremendous. I also met a guy just released from jail. God brought me just the right people to help me figure out the best possible message.

God uses us in other people's lives too. Many pastors can identify with this statement after a sermon: "It was like you were speaking just to me."

Most times, I think I'm speaking to myself and allowing others to listen. In this amazingly interconnected world of discipleship, sometimes you find yourself to be the one who is delivering wise counsel, even though you had no idea any of it was useful while preparing it.

God doesn't always answer our requests directly through divine revelation or a booming voice. He answers us through the voices of those in our communities.

You may be one of them.

Givers

He said to his disciples, "Have them sit down in groups of about fifty each." The disciples did so, and everyone sat down. Taking the five loaves and the two fish and looking

up to heaven, he gave thanks and broke them. Then he
gave them to the disciples to distribute to the people.

LUKE 9:14-16

When my wife, Barbie, battled with breast cancer and the side
effects of chemotherapy, I cannot tell you how many meals
showed up at our house. Easily more than one hundred. Someone
had sent out a link to an online sign-up calendar, and dozens
of people regularly brought us meals—nearly four a week for
more than seven months! We had to put a stop to them, mainly
because we were getting fat.

The following year, as happened to most people in 2009, our
finances ran bone dry. I couldn't get any steady work. I started to
pick up odd jobs like moving furniture, taking substitute teaching jobs, and folding clothes for retail. My wife picked up a second job doing monogramming in someone's home in addition
to her work at our church's preschool.

Some days, I worked from 7:00 a.m. to midnight, making
a little more than minimum wage each hour. We tightened our
belts and scraped by. Many cutbacks occurred, including presents, clothes, and food. Unfortunately, we had to miss a couple
of mortgage payments. As Christmas approached, we warned the
kids that we were heading into a very skimpy holiday.

It was anything but . . .

During the week of Christmas, something started to happen.
Three times, we heard the doorbell ring and went to answer, only
to find anonymous gifts had been dropped off—food, Starbucks,
and restaurant gift cards. Checks around $100 or $200 arrived.
Then, bigger checks showed up—$1,000, $2,000, and $3,500.

On Christmas Eve, as we started to open our few gifts, there
was a knock at the door.

Our student pastor and his wife entered with a huge turkey, stuffing, and all the fixings, plus a box full of presents. The student ministry and teachers all contributed to our cause. It was a Tiny Tim moment right out of Dickens!

Finally, we opened a letter dropped off by a friend of ours earlier in the day. It was someone we knew well, a professional golfer, but we hadn't crossed paths with him for a couple of years. He said that God had told him to sell his motorcycle and give the money to us. As our family gazed at the amount that night, we burst into tears (which was quite a feat for three teenage boys).

The check was for $5,000, the amount of delinquency on our mortgage. (The irony of the amount of this check has not escaped me while writing this book.)

During that time, God laid us on the hearts of more than thirty people, who, without consulting each other, all gave to our cause. We couldn't figure out how many of them knew about our struggle, which, for the most part, we had kept quiet outside of mentioning it to family and hinting at it in prayer requests to the staff and our home group. It was the most amazing blessing we had ever witnessed.

During our difficult times, our family frequently cries out one particular name for God: *Jehovah Jireh*. It means "The Lord Will Provide."[2] It comes from Genesis 22, when Abraham ascended Mount Moriah with his only son, Isaac, and prepared for a sacrifice. When Isaac asked where this sacrifice would come from, Abraham, confident, replied, *"Jehovah jireh"*—God will provide. And he did. God supplied a ram.

Even today, God provides in the form of meals, gift cards, and checks. He asks us to be the givers to our communities.

In our own situation, if we had opened our cupboards and miraculously found food, we would have been satisfied, but someone would have missed out on the blessing of blessing us. God could have electronically added money to our bank account, but instead, he provided through others.

God got the credit, but the givers got the blessing.

Servers

A Hershey's Kiss is about the simplest piece of candy you can imagine. A dollop of chocolate wrapped in silver aluminum foil—how hard can that be to make?

Visiting the Hershey's factory in Hershey, Pennsylvania, reveals the network that goes into that simple bite-size treat. Farmers process the cocoa bean. Loggers cut down the trees that make the paper for that little strip that sticks out the top of the Kiss. Chemists develop a preservative to keep the Kiss from spoiling. Machinists maintain the assembly plant. Union workers negotiate with the plant to keep everyone happy. Advertisers work to keep the concept of the Hershey's Kiss new and fresh in consumers' minds. Chain stores buy Hershey's Kisses in bulk, then distribute them to their individual outlets, where they are delivered by truckers, put on shelves by stockers, and rung up by clerks.

A simple Hershey's Kiss? Yeah, right. It takes a lot of people serving the same purpose to get a Hershey's Kiss to your mouth.

We see this during the Feeding of the Five Thousand when Jesus gave the disciples another important task—having the people sit in groups of fifty.

Jesus could have barked out these orders to the crowd; instead, he asked the disciples to make the announcements and to organize the groups.

He wanted them to work directly with the people—not to sit up on the mountain and look down on them, but to walk among them and touch them, getting down and dirty and serving them face-to-face.

As they passed out the fish sandwiches, the disciples saw thankful expressions; smiles; eyes filled with tears; children devouring the bread; pregnant mothers regaining their strength; and the elderly, once faint, now back on their feet.

Jesus provided the bread. The disciples took the bread to the groups or maybe the group leaders. The groups served one another.

Jesus could have multiplied the fish sandwiches and easily beamed them into the pockets and knapsacks of everyone within a half-mile radius. But he didn't do that. He asked the disciples to deliver the food to the people. Jesus could have set up a buffet, asking the people to make ten lines, turning the miracle into an enormous event at the Golden Corral. Instead, the disciples became waiters, delivering the food personally.

Even today, God always uses a number of people to get spiritual nourishment to communities: The writers of the Bible documented that Jesus is the truth. Pastors pass that truth on to their congregations. The community serves one another.

The group seating that Jesus requested conveys the idea of a church community. In fact, in this one miracle, Jesus started about three hundred small churches. That is a miracle!

These small communities are needed in our lives today. They remind us we are all in this together, working with each other toward a common goal. We need one another. No man or woman or child is an island. We were made for relationship, to teach, care for, and serve one another.

We design our churches around a stage where all eyes are forward, focused on the speaker or singer. Yes, we definitely need to share a common purpose and belief that comes from a common message uniting our hearts. But does it end there?

At the Feeding of the Five Thousand, Jesus started by being the center of attention, the main communicator, and then he bent those rows into circles. Why?

Andy Stanley at North Point Community Church says it best—"Life change happens in a circle, not sitting in rows."[3] It's when we get face-to-face, sharing our needs and resources with one another, that we see growth and healing in our lives.

These groups of fifty came together because Jesus gave them fish and bread; then they turned toward one another and passed on the blessing. They had the opportunity to practically love their neighbors and put into practice the principles Jesus had spoken about.

The body of Christ is called to serve others, both local and global. We are called to be the servers, so let's get serving.

The Promise of Community

In those huge fish-sandwich gatherings, God saw the need for smaller group settings. Today, a megachurch comprises five thousand people, but as churches get larger, they realize the need to get smaller.

Call it what you will—Sunday school, Bible study, cell groups, home groups, church—it's all the same: a community of people coming together to teach, care for, support, and encourage one another in smaller groups of ten, twenty, thirty, or at the most, fifty. Jesus led a small group of twelve, who in turn led other groups in their lifetimes. A large church needs to be organized with smaller units of care. One pastor cannot minister to hundreds or thousands effectively, but one pastor can inspire leaders to care for their own groups of ten or twenty.

It's a chain reaction—a spiritual-ripple theory.

LIFE IS A GROUP EFFORT.

As people sat in groups during the fish-sandwich buffets, I like to imagine what happened: They passed the bread and fish to each other. They shared their joy over the miracle. They talked about their needs. They laughed. They encouraged. Maybe they sang. They definitely felt connected. They became part of a historic moment.

Life is a group effort, requiring participation and involvement from others on all levels. We cannot survive in this world solely on our own efforts. God knows that, so he promises to bring others into our lives to advise us, provide for us, help us up when we've fallen, and carry us when we don't have enough strength.

God serves us community in the flesh-and-blood form of a body of believers. To receive this promise, you need to join a group where others are dining on fish sandwiches too.

Saying Grace

Lord, thank you for giving me the community of people in my life. Thank you for how they make me complete. Thank you that you speak to them when I'm in need to provide wisdom, provision, and servants' hearts. I pray I can be that kind of person to others, handing out blessings when they need them, being a conduit of love that begins with you.

Down-and-outers sit at GOD's *table*
and eat their fill.
Everyone on the hunt for God
is here, praising him.
"Live it up, from head to toe.
Don't ever quit!"

PSALM 22:26, THE MESSAGE

I will be fully satisfied as with the richest of foods;
with singing lips my mouth will praise you.

PSALM 63:5

#9

SATISFIED

The Promise of Fulfillment

They all ate and were satisfied.

MATTHEW 14:20, 15:37; MARK 6:42; LUKE 9:17

The people ate and were satisfied.

MARK 8:8

When they had all had enough to eat . . .

JOHN 6:12

IT'S DIFFICULT to find satisfaction in this world. Even the Rolling Stones understood that.

> *I can't get no satisfaction. . . .*
> *'Cause I try and I try and I try and I try.*[1]

What? Are you telling me that even Mick Jagger can't get no satisfaction? When he wrote this song with Keith Richards, he had tons of money, women in every city, and celebrity status. He was well liked, skinny as a mosquito's bicep, and . . . unfulfilled? What was going on? How could Mick have been unhappy?

When you read all the lyrics to the song, his lack of satisfaction resulted from listening to all the advice that the world tried to give him. The advertisements on TV told him the products he needed, but they did no good. His tours took him around the world where girls screamed and fainted and threw themselves at him, pleading for his autograph, and guess what—it all meant nothing.

Sounds like Mick read Ecclesiastes. You see, King Solomon knew something about stardom. He was the Bill Gates of the world when it came to money. He was the Albert Einstein of the world when it came to smarts. He was the Brad Pitt of the world when it came to women. He built several cities and a palace. He hung out with powerful diplomats, then married their daughters. He was the most famous king in the world.

Then he said . . .

"Meaningless! Meaningless!"
   says the Teacher.
"Utterly meaningless!
   Everything is meaningless."
ECCLESIASTES 1:2

Solomon goes on to tell us in Ecclesiastes that

- work doesn't satisfy;
- people come and go out of our lives;
- life is routine . . . tiresome;
- we want more, but more doesn't fill us up;
- there's nothing new—been there, done that; and
- we will all die and be forgotten.

Solomon could have recorded Ecclesiastes as a song and called it "(I Can't Get No) Satisfaction" and made millions of dollars more, but that wouldn't have helped any. After all the fame and number one hits, Solomon still would have ended up saying, "What's the use?"

This is not a statement of depression by Solomon and Mick Jagger but a realization of truth. When we exist on a steady diet of worldliness, we never get full.

That's not the case for the people who received the fish sandwiches. Each account makes the same observation: Everybody who took a bite of a fish sandwich was satisfied. Everybody had enough. Does this mean their stomachs were full? Sure, absolutely.

They were not only full but also fulfilled. Satisfaction was mentioned in every retelling of the story. The Greek word used here in the passages for "satisfied" is *chortazó*, which means not only to feed but also to feed to the feeling of fullness. The word has a deeper, emotional aspect of fulfilling one's desires.[2] Have you ever eaten a meal and said you would never have to eat again? It's more than just feeling Thanksgiving-stuffed—it's having your soul stuffed too.

How do we get that satisfaction in our lives when we sense God's fulfillment daily, when we don't get hungry and thirst for more? Appreciation, trust, and focusing on our needs, not wants.

Satisfaction Comes by Appreciation

Have you ever gone out to eat with one of those people who put in a special order?

> I'd like a turkey sandwich, but I want boneless,
> skinless, all-white turkey meat only, with provolone
> and ficaccio cheese, no American, on a fat-free
> croissant, baked slowly in the oven for nine minutes at

350 degrees, removed and placed on a steel warming rack for five minutes, not six. Add two (vine-ripened) tomato slices, a quarter inch thick, and one leaf of romaine lettuce grown in California and harvested no later than January or February, and coat one side with pesto mayonnaise and the other with olive oil (extra virgin). Then slice it delicately with a serrated knife.

You know the type. What's on the menu is never enough or never right. They must have it their way. It's a pattern of behavior seen clearly throughout the Bible. Take the Israelites in the desert, for example:

> The rabble with them began to crave other food, and again the Israelites started wailing and said, "If only we had meat to eat! We remember the fish we ate in Egypt at no cost—also the cucumbers, melons, leeks, onions and garlic. But now we have lost our appetite; we never see anything but this manna!"
> NUMBERS 11:4-6

Even when the Israelites wandered the desert because of their disobedience, God still provided for them, despite their complaints for more and better and different. Their clothes never wore out, and they received food and water. The food came in the form of manna, a bread-like substance that came down to the ground with the dew at night. It was Instant Bread—just gather and bake. Water flowed when Moses banged on a rock with his staff, much like we do when the Coke machine doesn't give us the can we paid for.

However, the manna got repetitive, and the Israelites put in a special order. "We want meat!" they cried. God rolled his eyes and shook his head.

"Okay, meat it is."

A wind blew in tons of quail. The Israelites killed the birds and ate, but while the meat was still in their mouths, seconds from being swallowed, God got angry and sent a severe plague their way.[3]

Now what happened? Did God just snap? Though the reason is not clearly stated, a few possibilities exist. Maybe . . .

- *They turned into gluttons.* God struck them with a plague, it says, while the quail meat was in their mouths. Were they eating like gluttonous pigs? Were their attitudes "Quick, eat, because we have no idea if God will ever provide for us again"? Did they rip into the quail while it was still raw?

- *They did not pray before they ate.* Maybe these Israelites were more concerned about their hunger than thanking God. "Food. Eat. Now!"

- *They felt they deserved better quality.* Heavenly Manna and Rock Water were on the menu. Wind-Swept Quail was the chef's special. Bread was a simple staple of their diet. Quail was a luxury. The Israelites felt they were entitled to get the very best. "Hey, we're the Chosen Ones! The regular menu is not good enough for us!" Bread kept them humble and close to God. Quail made them feel like snobby, quail-eating elite, with pinky fingers erected high in the air. God hates that kind of arrogance.

- *They were unhappy with the order.* "Yes, we would like the quail gently plucked, then rubbed in butter, sprinkled with herbs, and cooked over the fire for twenty-two minutes—not twenty-one, not twenty-three . . ." You get the idea. Ordering God around would have positioned them as disgruntled customers, not appreciative receivers.

Jesus started the fish-sandwich buffet with appreciation for the food by looking up and thanking his Father. The entire miracle began with appreciation, then ended with satisfaction.

So how does appreciation lead to satisfaction?

Once, Jesus healed ten lepers.

> One of them, when he saw he was healed, came back, praising God in a loud voice. He threw himself at Jesus' feet and thanked him—and he was a Samaritan.
>
> Jesus asked, "Were not all ten cleansed? Where are the other nine? Has no one returned to give praise to God except this foreigner?" Then he said to him, "Rise and go; your faith has made you well."
>
> LUKE 17:15-19

Only one showed appreciation. Only one gave thanks. Notice Jesus' response to the one: "Your faith has made you well." Wasn't the leper already well? Wasn't he as well as the other nine in leprosy-free bodies?

Jesus seemed to say that this one who worshiped God and gave thanks received an extra dose of wellness. The other nine left physically healed, but were they spiritually "well"? Was their faith healed too, deep down in their hearts, where they found satisfaction? The thankful leper got something more fulfilling.

A lack of appreciation always breeds sin. Eve didn't appreciate her situation and brought sin into the world. David wanted more wives and paid for it. Judas didn't like the current state of affairs and betrayed a friend. Dissatisfaction doesn't like God's plan and looks for an alternate plan. Then, at some point, the person realizes their plan only took them further away from God, who is the true source of all satisfaction.

A LACK OF APPRECIATION ALWAYS BREEDS SIN.

The only way those consuming the fish sandwiches felt satisfied that day was because they were thankful that an extraordinary meal had been served especially for them.

Satisfaction Comes by Trust

So you've placed your order in the restaurant. Now you must wait. (By the way, why do they call the server's job "waiting tables" when the customers are doing all the waiting?)

Waiting is the hardest part, as you watch trays of food pass by, as those arrogant cows ahead of you chow down on their meals while you sit there starving like an orphan from a Dickens novel, begging for a morsel. Then your food finally arrives, and you, too, chow down like an arrogant cow . . . and someone else must wait after you.

From the moment you order until the moment your food arrives, an eternity seems to pass. You're picturing food in your mind, which alerts your stomach lining and activates your drooling glands. Then you're *really* hungry.

When we order our food, truth is, we want it delivered *Star Trek* style. Remember when in the old, original series, Kirk walked into the mess hall and pushed a button, and a fully prepared tray came out of the food computer?[4]

Restaurants aren't quite like that, but they want you to get your food quickly. However, certain obstacles cannot be avoided:

- the distance the waiter must travel from your table to the kitchen, hopefully without being interrupted;
- the hour the order was placed (lunch rush versus 4:00 "early-bird" dinner);
- the number of orders placed previously;
- the number of chefs on duty (hopefully no one called in sick or quit);
- the amount of food needed for one order;
- the preparedness of those orders;
- the complexity of your order (salad versus prime rib); and
- the distance back to your table with the order.

God hears disgruntled customers all the time. Many ask, "Where's that thing I want? What's taking so long? God, you don't care! Who's in charge here?"

Let's imagine you are the 14,956th guy at the Feeding of Fifteen Thousand men, women, and children. People start organizing into groups of fifty. You wonder, *What's going on?* Then, out of nowhere, you see this delicious food being delivered by the disciples. The smell of freshly baked bread seeps into your nostrils. Saliva builds. Suddenly, you realize you're hungry. Now you get impatient. "Where's my fish sandwich?" As you look out over the crowd and count the groups, it hits you . . . your group will be last.

Then you mumble under your breath, "Why is everyone getting served ahead of me? I'm hungry *now!*"

We do the same thing with God. We have a need and we want a solution *now*, but sometimes the solution needs time to get in place.

Look at everything that had to happen at the fish-sandwich miracle before food settled in the stomachs of the last group to be served:

- The disciples and Jesus had a meeting over the problem.
- The disciples asked around for solutions, then scrounged up some bread and fish.
- They had another meeting to discuss the failure of acquiring enough food for everyone. Jesus offered his solution.
- They organized the fifteen thousand people into small groups of fifty.
- Jesus multiplied the bread and fish, then distributed it to the disciples.
- The disciples handed it out to the groups of fifty.
- One person then handed it out to the other forty-nine.

I know sometimes in my life I feel like the 14,956th guy at the fish-sandwich experience of fifteen thousand, watching the wave of blessing spread from person to person, feeling like I do when I see waiters serving people who sat down after me. "Hey, I was here first!"

Just as we have to trust that the restaurant's employees are doing everything they can within the demands of their schedule to get our orders to the table, we have to trust that God is "cooking up something" in the kitchen. Things need to fall into place. People may have to get situated. Hearts changed. Eyes opened. Economies shifted. Resources found. Relationships developed.

It takes time.

When we don't have it now, we want it even more. During

those times, God wants us to trust him more. Trust his timing and trust what's coming.

We have to trust that God's answer is coming, because we owe God our obedience. Believing in him is the most basic act of obedience. We can trust that God's answer is coming because his character and history point to an inevitable answer.

Just wait . . . patiently, appreciatively.

Without trust, impatience creeps in. When impatience creeps in, we lose our satisfaction with life because we don't have in our possession right this minute what we see others getting. We start to feel we are entitled. We lose our humility.

If all that happens, we can never be fulfilled.

We must trust God's timing to get us what we need, when we need it, or we'll never be truly fulfilled.

Satisfaction Comes by Getting What You Need, Not What You Want

> *You can't always get what you want;*
> *But if you try sometimes, you just might find . . .*
> *You get what you need.*[5]
>
> "YOU CAN'T ALWAYS GET WHAT YOU WANT,"
> THE ROLLING STONES

There's Mick at it again. Don't you just wonder what was going on in the lives of the songwriters—Mick Jagger and Keith Richards—that would motivate them to write another "Where's my fulfillment?" song four years after getting no satisfaction?

Mick makes the right point—we don't always get what we want, but we should try to get what we need. Give one of the world's most highly successful rock bands some credit. Rock stars get everything they want, whether they need it or not, and yet, the Rolling Stones didn't write about the accumulation of fast cars, Benjamins (that's one-hundred-dollar bills for you old people), and bling (that's jewelry). The Stones actually saw the difference between wants and needs.

So, what's the difference?

Merriam-Webster.com lists one definition for a *need* as "a physiological or psychological requirement for the well-being of an organism."[6] It is something that is essential in order to live. Things like food, shelter, clothing, relationships.

One definition for a *want* is "the state or condition of not having any or enough of something."[7] The word focuses more on desire, wishing, and longing for something. For the sake of our argument, *wants* are special orders.

You may want a Ferrari so you can get to work, but all you need is bus transportation. You may want a beautiful model by your side, but all you need is a friend. You may want pan-seared yellow-fin tuna served with a white bean, artichoke, and bacon ragout; garlic-smothered broccoli rabe; veal with balsamic reduction; and an herb-Dijon aioli from Emeril's Restaurant. But a can of tuna is really all you need.

I put a twenty-four-hour waiting period on my wants. I'll search online, find stuff I like, then set it aside until I return later. One of the greatest components of Amazon.com is the Wish List. I can put something on my Wish List and buy it later, when I have the money. Sometimes, though, I return to that list and wonder, *What was I thinking?*

Many wants appear ridiculous when you go back and look at them later. A need is never ridiculous or crazy—it's essential in its most basic form.

If you have exactly what you need and appreciate what you have, the wants don't weigh you down. The wants distract us, and we get lost. The wants make us feel empty. But if we have what we need and know that's all we need, we feel fulfilled, satisfied, blessed.

When a desire comes to mind, ask yourself, *Do I need it, or do I just want it?*

The apostle Paul understood something about needs:

> I am not saying this because I am in need, for I have
> learned to be content whatever the circumstances.
> I know what it is to be in need, and I know what it is to
> have plenty. I have learned the secret of being content
> in any and every situation, whether well fed or hungry,
> whether living in plenty or in want. I can do all this
> through him who gives me strength.
> PHILIPPIANS 4:11-13

Paul wrote this in prison. Even in a place that denied all wants and needs, he still proclaimed he had all he needed.

- He's happy no matter what happens.
- He knows what it's like to have nothing.
- He knows what it's like to have more than enough.
- He gets all his strength—no matter the circumstance—by the power of Christ.

Those experiencing the fish sandwiches understood what Paul understood.

They were fulfilled through the food they had received.

They were fulfilled through the relationships they had developed.

They were fulfilled by experiencing the power of God.

And aren't these all the things we truly need—food, relationships, God, worship?

Filled with right attitudes and thankful hearts, everyone present at the miraculous feedings walked away satisfied.

Mick is right: We may not always get what we want.

But, thank God, Jesus promises to give us what we need.

The Promise of Fulfillment

Sometimes we think Santa Claus has a bigger heart than God. We think Santa Claus is that guy who wants to give you everything on your list, while God wants you to live in poverty because it's good for your humility. That's not entirely true, but it's what we think.

God knows our nature better than Santa. God knows having more does not always satisfy more, so he gives us exactly what we need.

> SOMETIMES WE THINK SANTA CLAUS HAS A BIGGER HEART THAN GOD.

When my kids were young, I examined their Christmas lists with disappointment every year. Lots of expensive stuff I knew I couldn't afford, and much of it was useless. I knew it would decorate the floor on Christmas Day, but by Boxing Day in Canada (that's December 26), it would be as outdated as a Tickle Me Elmo.

Despite my practicality and discernment, please understand this: I wanted to give it all to them! Every bit of it and one of every color!

However, we edited down our children's wish lists because we knew them better than they knew themselves. For each item, we asked ourselves,

- Is it the type of thing they will use over and over?
- Will it take them away from school or family?
- What about storage? Do they have room for it?
- How will it impact their brothers?

In other words, Was it really good for them?

We knew what they really needed (underwear, shirts, sneakers), but we also blessed them with what they wanted, those things that brought smiles to their faces and joy to their hearts, though sometimes those reactions were short-lived.

Sometimes we threw in the unexpected. One year, we surprised the boys with a golden retriever named Roxy. They didn't ask for her, but they got her. My youngest son, Carson, said, "Roxy was the best Christmas I ever received." Is it possible to like some things we never asked for?

Don't you think God does the same with our lists, asking the important questions,

- Is it useful for them?
- Will it bring them closer to me or further away?
- How does it fit in their lives?
- How will it affect others?

And doesn't he want to throw in some unexpected surprises—things we never wanted but now realize we always needed?

Trust God to give you what you need, when you need it—and in the way he wants to deliver it. He knows what's best.

The Lord will guide you always;
    he will satisfy your needs in a sun-scorched land
    and will strengthen your frame.

You will be like a well-watered garden,
    like a spring whose waters never fail.
ISAIAH 58:11

There's only one place to go for complete satisfaction, and that's God. If you're running dry, losing strength, and lacking fruitfulness, he won't fail you.

Saying Grace

Lord, thank you for all that you have given me. I've truly been blessed. I trust you to provide what I need. I know you are working on those things right now. They will come when I'm ready . . . when you're ready. I will find satisfaction only through you and your promises. Help me to discern between what I need and what I want.

GOD will order a blessing on your barns and workplaces; he'll bless you in the land that GOD, your God, is giving you.

DEUTERONOMY 28:8, *THE MESSAGE*

#10

LEFTOVERS

The Promise of Blessing

When they had all had enough to eat, he said to his disciples, "Gather the pieces that are left over. Let nothing be wasted." So they gathered them and filled twelve baskets with the pieces of the five barley loaves left over by those who had eaten.

JOHN 6:12-13

Afterward the disciples picked up seven basketfuls of broken pieces that were left over.

MARK 8:8

MULTIPLICATION ROCK on Saturday mornings was the math version of *Schoolhouse Rock! Multiplication Rock* featured catchy little tunes to educate kids about the power of multiplication. The show included songs for all numbers up to twelve. There was even one called "My Hero, Zero."

Now, what's so heroic about the number zero? Who would want zero? Zero is nothing. Until you realized the point of the song:

But place a zero after 1,
And you've got yourself a 10.
See how important that is?[1]

Two zeros and you have 100.

Three—1,000.

Four—10,000.

You get the idea. Zero means nothing until you write it behind another number and . . . *kerpow!*—it's now worth ten times the previous amount.

There's power in math, and God uses math to bless our lives. (Many of you taking Algebra VI just groaned.)

To bless means simply to make happy. I'm sure you know what *happy* means. It has many other expressions—*content, joyful, gleeful, cheerful, blissful,* and of course, *tickled pink.*

Happiness is what we seek on a daily basis. I know of no one who looks for sadness, mourning, or pain. Certainly, some seem programmed toward negativity. They're always depressed, choosing to swim in a sea of their own misery. But I believe even the Debbie Downers and Barry Bummers are really trying to find happiness; they're just having a hard time hanging on to it or accepting that they deserve it.

God does not intend that our lives be wretched. He promises to bless us. Those blessings come in varying degrees of intensity that are based on the way God does the math.

Rocks or Bread?

It's the Great Pumpkin, Charlie Brown contains one of my favorite lines. Charlie Brown, clad in a disastrous multi-eyed ghost costume, is going door-to-door with his friends to collect treats. As the children hold out their bags, a homeowner dumps several goodies into each one.

Gathering at the sidewalk, the children compare their haul.

"I got five pieces of candy."

"I got a chocolate bar."

"I got a quarter."

Charlie Brown holds up his prize. "I got a rock."[2]

At every house, Charlie Brown adds one more rock to his quarry collection. You have to wonder, *What were these homeowners thinking?* Why would they throw a rock into a bag of treats? Why would they take one look at the funny-looking, round-headed ghost, then feel impelled to skip the popcorn ball, fudge bar, pack of gum, or cold, hard cash and give him a big ol' hunk of granite?

The stupid kid deserves it . . .

That'll teach him that you don't always get what you want . . .

Rocks aren't all bad. They make great paperweights.

Rocks are rocks, especially when you want some candy. They are about as far from candy as you can get. We would never give a rock to a starving person.

Or how about promising guests broiled snapper as you plop a fried python on their plate? Unheard of? Unspeakable? Who would be so callous?

Jesus made an interesting promise in Matthew 7:9-11, using the concept of fish and bread:

> Which of you, if your son asks for bread, will give him a stone? Or if he asks for a fish, will give him a snake? If you, then, though you are evil, know how to give good gifts to your children, how much more will your Father in heaven give good gifts to those who ask him!

We know God hears our prayers and loves us, but to think he'll actually do something nice for us . . . that's another story.

We believe that if we ask God for help, he'll send a problem. Or if we ask for transportation, he'll send a rusty ol' scooter. Or if we ask for directions, God will send a tiny compass. We believe God's more interested in teaching us lessons on humility and sacrifice than giving us anything substantial, delicious, or pleasing.

WE BELIEVE GOD IS IN THE ROCK-GIVING MINISTRY MORE THAN HE'S IN THE BREAD-GIVING MINISTRY.

We believe God is in the rock-giving ministry more than he's in the bread-giving ministry.

At the Feeding of the Fish Sandwiches, imagine Jesus handing out rocks or releasing poisonous snakes onto the hungry and unsuspecting group of fifteen thousand people.

> *Crowd*: "Jesus, we're hungry."
> *Jesus*: "Tasty rocks and poisonous snakes for you!"
> *Crowd (running for their lives)*:
> "AHHHHHHHHHHHHHHHH!!!"

I can see the stiff-necked, penny-pinching, polyester-suited Bible scholar expounding on that one from the pulpit:

> Obviously these people were sinners, and rocks and snakes came down as judgment for their sins. God doesn't give us what we want. God gives us what we deserve! Amen?

Those in the audience nod their heads in agreement. On the outside, it sounds right. On the inside, they're scared to death. They'll never ask God for anything ever again.

Especially for something as simple as a piece of bread or a tasty fish.

Back in the '90s, an anonymous Florida resident started a $150,000 ad campaign featuring one-liners from God as a sort of public service announcement. After that, it grew to ten thousand billboards and $15 million in ad space.[3] Some of the messages read,

- What part of "Thou Shalt Not . . ." didn't you understand? —God
- Keep using my name in vain and I'll make rush hour longer. —God
- We need to talk. —God
- You think it's hot here? —God
- My way is the highway. —God
- Have you read my #1 best seller? There will be a test. —God
- I don't question your existence. —God
- Do you have any idea where you're going? —God
- That "Love Thy Neighbor" thing—I meant it. —God
- Don't make me come down there. —God[4]

The tone of the ads got people's attention, but as the campaign grew, the messages came off as harsh and unloving, feeding into the world's portrayal of God as a composite of all the worst teachers, preachers, parents, bullies, and judges wrapped up into one divine being who doesn't want to bless us but instead wants to curse us, burden us, and slap us upside the head. However, God is nothing like that.

Nowhere in the Bible do we see God enjoying the subtraction of blessing. When he dealt with the Israelites' rebelliousness before they entered the Promised Land, he did so patiently. During the time of the Judges and after the time of King Solomon . . . well, actually, he was mad at them all the time, it seemed—his own people for whom he had worked so hard to get into the Promised Land, only to see them break his rules. As judgment, God sent two nations to fight against the divided kingdom, taking out his anger on his people.

This happened over a period of four hundred to six hundred years—not exactly God losing his cool or flying off the handle! Rather, he warned the Israelites over and over and over so he wouldn't have to remove his blessing and protection. He did everything possible to keep it from happening: calling on the people to look to him and seek him, sending prophets to encourage them. Hundreds of years later, he allowed judgment to occur.

These incidents paint God as anything but a vengeful, angry God. He's patient and loving. He wants to bless, but he must step in when people need reminders that he is God.

When we do seek him on a daily basis, following his commandments, we find God adds easy and simple blessings to our lives. Nothing outrageous—not always fish sandwiches falling from the sky, but maybe pieces of bread or cans of tuna fish. We just have to look for them in the daily moments:

That five dollars you found in your pants pocket . . .

The car starting on a cold morning . . .

Someone who arrives to open the door when your hands are full . . .

Enough food for tomorrow . . .

A smile from your child . . .

A phone call from a friend . . .

Not another rock added to your bag of burdens. Not another snake chasing your weary soul.

Nothing extravagant or expensive, just timely and needed, simple and appreciated.

And if you really turn on your blessings radar, those singular blessings—one here, one there—begin to add up. In a day, a zero is added to that one. In a week, maybe two zeros.

The Feedings of the Five Thousand and Four Thousand were really just one more meal added to the many meals these people would be eating in their lifetimes. Eight hours later, they were all hungry again. It's simple math. It's not as if everyone present never ate again for the rest of their lives. The blessing was *one good meal*, totally satisfying, absolutely free, especially delicious during a sunny day on the shore, far from any place that was open for business.

If you take a moment to add up all the little blessings, you will find that God adds a number of zeros to your life.

God's Multiplication Table

I liked math in school. There, I said it. I would have never confessed such a thing back then, because saying you liked math around teenagers labeled you a rebel, a weirdo . . . a nerd. This was before being a nerd was cool.

But math worked for me. The problems were like puzzles. Mysteries. "Sherlock Holmes and the Secret of the X Minus Y."

However, now that I've grown up, I see very little need for a lot of the math I learned. Calculus? Never. Geometry? Maybe while picking furniture or fabric patterns. Trigonometry? I forget what that was.

Twenty years after graduating from high school, I saw one of my high school teachers in church. I said hello, told him my name, and asked him to remind me what he had taught.

"Algebra," he replied. Not even thinking, I said, "I've never used algebra in my life." He laughed, thankfully, and responded, "Neither have I."

But the math tools of adding and subtracting I use every day. Not a day goes by that I don't add or subtract something, from hours to mileage to the correct change.

The next-most-practiced mathematical exercise may be multiplication. It's the most promising of all the simple-math operations. Subtracting and dividing mean I am receiving less of something. Adding is good, but it is limited. Multiplication— now there's where the abundance is at.

Who wouldn't want their income doubled or their investments tripled? Who doesn't desire twice as many points or four times as much pie? Would you rather have another three dollars an hour or three times as much an hour?

Try this word problem: Would you rather work for $100 a day for one month or one cent the first day and double that amount every day for thirty days?

At $100 a day, you will get $3,000 by day thirty ($100 \times 30 = 3,000$).

On the other hand . . .

Day	Amount per day ($)
1	.01
2	.02
3	.04
4	.08
5	.16
6	.32
7	.64
8	1.28
9	2.56
10	5.12
11	10.24
12	20.48

13	40.96
14	81.92
15	163.84
16	327.68
17	655.36
18	1,310.72
19	2,621.44
20	5,242.88
21	10,485.76
22	20,971.52
23	41,943.04
24	83,886.08
25	167,772.16
26	335,544.32
27	671,088.64
28	1,342,177.28
29	2,684,354.56
30	5,368,709.12

Your grand total for the month is $10,737,418.23.

Now what do you think of multiplication? Many of you thought, *What good is a penny, even if that amount is doubled every day?* Not quite halfway into the month, you're thinking, *I'm getting ripped off. All this time, and only 40 bucks for a day of work. I could be making $100 a day!*

All of a sudden, 40 becomes 80, and 80 becomes 160. Then it takes off, and soon you're making 5 million dollars in one day!

God loves multiplication too.

In Genesis, after the Flood, he commanded Noah, his sons, and the animals who were spared to be fruitful and multiply.[5]

In Exodus, he watched as the Israelites multiplied greatly in number; then he adopted them as his own.[6]

He multiplied the signs and wonders he displayed to the Israelites, so they would know he was God.

At Pentecost, one sermon inspired three thousand people to receive Christ.[7]

He also multiplied fish and bread to the nth power and fed thousands.

God isn't all about giving us one or two. That's good, simple math, but he's also about hundreds and thousands. Big-time multiplication.

Miraculously feeding twelve disciples would not make the headlines. Feeding thousands of people will make the news every time.

We have a hard time multiplying our efforts in life. We promise to work twice as hard to make twice as much money. If I drive twice as fast, I'll get there in half the time. Right?

When we double our efforts in one area, we must subtract and divide in another. More time at work means less time with family and friends. Outside factors also minimize our efforts. Economy, war, supply, demand, exhaustion, sickness, police with radar guns . . . all divide our efforts.

Simply working twice as hard does not mean twice the return. In that way, it's not like math—easy, clean, logical. Two times two always equals four, except in life.

Life is more like those complicated problems you see scrawled on chalkboards in movies like *A Beautiful Mind* and *Good Will Hunting*—equations that only Albert Einstein and Stephen Hawking would understand.

$$33.1 + 24(8 \times 25) \, / \, pi - 92 \times 1291233.345 + abc - pdq \times 989 = x$$

It's not easy, but God understands life's formulas. He's a brilliant mathematician who can do more than just add a little here and there. He wants to go to the nth power in your life.

How much more will your Father in heaven give good
gifts to those who ask him!

MATTHEW 7:11

God miraculously fed the five thousand / four thousand for
this reason: In an unpredictable world filled with many variables,
the only way to see the multiplication of
our efforts and sense a greater satisfaction,
fulfillment, and joy in life is to multiply
God into the equation.

Of course, you can't be doing something he doesn't want you to do. The
Israelites learned this the hard way. Sin
divides and subtracts from the blessings

**SIN DIVIDES AND
SUBTRACTS FROM THE
BLESSINGS IN OUR
LIVES, BECAUSE GOD
IS NOT PRESENT.**

in our lives, because God is not present in sin. If you lovingly and
obediently follow God, you'll see widespread blessings.

When people talk about the feedings, they always use the
same expression: *Jesus* multiplied *the loaves and fishes*. The formula here is

5 loaves × x = thousands of loaves

2 fish × x = thousands of fish

What is the X in each of these equations? Jesus.

Merriam-Webster.com defines $X factor$ as "a circumstance,
quality, or person that has a strong but unpredictable influence."[8]

Jesus is the X factor, that mysterious and wonderful algebraic
number that intensifies the original.

Jesus is not x = 0, because that would mean anything times

Jesus turns to nothing. It would be as if the disciples had handed Jesus five loaves and two fish, only to witness Jesus holding them up to the sky, thanking his Father, and eating them himself, leaving zero loaves and zero fish for everyone else.

Jesus is not $x = 1$, because that would mean anything times Jesus is no greater than the original (really, just the same). So if the disciples had handed Jesus five loaves and two fish, then Jesus would have held them up to the sky, thanked his Father, and handed them right back to the disciples. The number one says Jesus makes no difference.

But that wasn't the case. The disciples handed Jesus five loaves and two fish, and multiplication happened.

What about your life? Could multiplication happen if you handed it over to Jesus? We try to double a recipe, and it flops. Not so with God.

Maybe $x = 2$, where Jesus doubles your efforts.

Or $x = 3$, when he makes your life three times as fruitful.

In the formula for the Feeding of the Five Thousand, Jesus equals more than a thousand times more of each ingredient he was given.

So if you give what you have over to Jesus, he is capable of producing two, three, or a thousand times more than what you originally had.

He is the God of Multiplication. The God of How Much More. What in your life could be a thousand times more effective if you just let God do the math and add some zeros to your formula?

This is the God of eternity. He exists and thinks in a reality of infinity. Time is eternal. Life is never ending. His ultimate gift to us is time multiplied by forever in a place of eternal joy.

God's multiplication rocks!

God Uses Remainders

Remainders are those numbers that don't figure equally into the equation. They are the fraction or the decimal point that sits off to the side, separate from the whole numbers God uses.

For example, 5 goes into 11 twice with a remainder of 1. There's nothing wrong with the 1—it's a really good 1—it's just . . . left over.

Tupperware is a billion-dollar company. It was founded in 1946, during the postwar era, when inventor Earl Tupper dedicated his wartime plastics for consumer use. His contribution to the world? Airtight seals. With World War II over, the suburbs grew, and women became more home focused. Home Parties began so women could see demonstrations of this sealing method. Now the company operates in nearly one hundred countries, with product lines in such places as Tunisia, the Philippines, and Uruguay. You can even buy products specific to regions, like a Kimchi Keeper or a Japanese Bento Box.[9]

What built this company? Leftovers.

Many claim that day-after-Thanksgiving turkey tastes pretty good, if not better than Thanksgiving Day turkey. It has something to do with the meat soaking up the juices from the stuffing and gravy. I doubt scientists have done studies on that kind of thing. Plus, the leftovers can evolve into other meals, such as turkey sandwiches, turkey casserole, turkey tetrazzini, or simple right-out-of-the-refrigerator-and-into-your-mouth turkey.

The God of Multiplication likes leftovers, as we see at the Feeding of the Five Thousand:

When they had all had enough to eat, he said to his disciples, "Gather the pieces that are left over. Let nothing be wasted."

JOHN 6:12

Were the leftovers a result of bad math? Did someone forget to carry the 1? If God can't make an accurate head count, I don't want him planning my next banquet. "Aw gee, I'm sorry; we overbooked by five hundred people!" Now, the God who pulled fish and bread out of a hat had to know how many people were sitting before him. Why did he have remainders?

Remainders are a sign of God's overflowing blessing into our lives. God pours blessing up to the rim and over. He tops off our tanks. His love spills out from our hearts and all around us.

How much more?

Have you ever watched a worker prepare your food at a fast-food restaurant? Some items are carefully weighed and measured, so everyone gets the same amount—2.2 ounces. They seem to hold back when they sprinkle cheese on the top, and you want to say, "Could you add a little more?"

"Sorry, regulations say everyone gets exactly .6 milligrams of cheese."

Sure, it's the rule, but BLESS ME with .4 more milligrams of cheese!

A friend of mine was getting a sub sandwich and asked the food preparer to put on some extra black olives.

The response: "Sorry, we're saving those for the other customers."

He yelled back, "I *am* the other customer!"

So they gathered [the leftovers] and filled twelve baskets with the pieces of the five barley loaves left over by those who had eaten.

JOHN 6:13

The people ate and were satisfied. Afterward the disciples picked up seven basketfuls of broken pieces that were left over.

MARK 8:8

So, if everyone ate to satisfaction, why were there leftovers? One reason points back to Elisha's miracle.

"How can I set this before a hundred men?" his servant asked.

But Elisha answered, "Give it to the people to eat. For this is what the LORD says: 'They will eat and have some left over.'" Then he set it before them, and they ate and had some left over, according to the word of the LORD.

2 KINGS 4:43-44

Elisha made enough for leftovers. Jesus purposely realigned himself with Elisha the great prophet by saying, "If Elisha can make leftovers, so can I."

But did the leftovers have a purpose?

Maybe the disciples stuffed their pockets for a long journey ahead—food they needed later, when they were worn out and hungry and needed to tap into a previous blessing.

Maybe they handed it out to beggars on the road—blessing others with their own blessing.

Whatever happened, none of it went to waste. I'm sure birds consumed the crumbs and crusts that had fallen to the ground. God does say he takes care of "the birds of the air."[10] Maybe this is how he does it. I think every little bit of that miraculous event went to some good use.

God's Return Policy

When God blesses us to overflowing, we need to pick up our blessings and do something with them—hand them out, spread them around, give them to others—because when it comes to leftovers, God has a clear and definite return policy.

Jesus told all sorts of parables about workers who were given something and then squandered what they got.

In one story,[11] a landowner gave three servants $6,000[12] each and told them to do something with it. One of them took that investment and turned it into $60,000. The other's investment became $30,000. The last one did nothing. The landowner got pretty mad at the last guy. Why?

Remember, for starters, these poor servants were given $6,000! That was the multiplication blessing! But the blessing did not stop there. The landowner was not saying, "Bless you, my workers. Sit around and get fat!" He said, "I'm blessing you; now go out and create more blessing."

BLESSINGS DO NOT STOP WITH US. THEY CONTINUE ON THROUGH US.

God wants a return for his blessing.

It's the difference between a sponge and a cup. I'm not a sponge, soaking up blessing. I'm a cup, taking it in and pouring it out.

Blessings are not gifts to be consumed but resources to put to good use.

Blessings do not stop with us. They continue on through us.

When God multiplies in your life, hand it out, spill it over, return it to those around you. If you receive a blessing, donate a little extra to your favorite charity, give some time at a local homeless shelter, or use your talents at church.

[Jesus said,] "Give, and it will be given to you. A good measure, pressed down, shaken together and running over, will be poured into your lap. For with the measure you use, it will be measured to you."

LUKE 6:38

Remember the baskets that held the leftovers? Does the number of leftover baskets have any significance? After the miracles, Jesus spoke to his disciples about those leftovers, saying,

"When I broke the five loaves for the five thousand, how many basketfuls of pieces did you pick up?"

"Twelve," they replied.

"And when I broke the seven loaves for the four thousand, how many basketfuls of pieces did you pick up?"

They answered, "Seven."

He said to them, "Do you still not understand?"

MARK 8:19-21

Jesus never explained the significance, but he wanted the disciples to understand. So what did the number of baskets mean?

Let's go back to the target audience for each of the miraculous feedings.

Remember the Feeding of the Five Thousand was primarily for the Jews. The Jews came from twelve tribes (twelve baskets).

The Feeding of the Four Thousand was aimed at Gentiles (non-Jews) primarily. People in Jesus' time believed that the Gentiles came from seven nations (seven baskets) that once occupied the Promised Land. Moses said to the Israelites before they entered the land that would become Israel,

> When the LORD your God brings you into the land
> you are entering to possess and drives out before you
> many nations—the Hittites, Girgashites, Amorites,
> Canaanites, Perizzites, Hivites and Jebusites, seven
> nations larger and stronger than you . . .
> DEUTERONOMY 7:1

Those seven nations were the opposition, the outsiders, those not like the Jews.

So what do the baskets mean?

Twelve baskets—bless those like you
Seven baskets—bless those not like you

It seems Jesus was saying, "I have so much sustenance in me that I cannot feed only you but will also give you leftovers to distribute to all the Jews and all the Gentiles in the world!"

From the leftovers, Jesus made a case for missions through the number of baskets. Take what you have and spread the blessing to other people less fortunate, whether they are your friends or your enemies, those across the street or around the world, those who speak your language or not.

I love the adventure of mission trips, the opportunities to meet people not like me and bless them in return. I always come back realizing how blessed I am as an American.

But I also return knowing more about God through their examples, especially when it comes to overflowing blessings. The people we meet on mission trips give out of their poverty, while I give out of my abundance—just as in the story where Jesus observes the poor widow:

> Jesus sat down opposite the place where the offerings were put and watched the crowd putting their money into the temple treasury. Many rich people threw in large amounts. But a poor widow came and put in two very small copper coins, worth only a few cents.
>
> Calling his disciples to him, Jesus said, "Truly I tell you, this poor widow has put more into the treasury than all the others. They all gave out of their wealth; but she, out of her poverty, put in everything—all she had to live on."
> MARK 12:41-44

I remember speaking at a home church in Santiago de Cuba, in a room decorated in outdated and dilapidated furniture. Their wall decorations included a hubcap and McDonald's Happy Meal toys. Afterward, I slipped into the kitchen of the host family. As we sat on a torn and rickety couch, they brought out a plate of cookies and Cuban coffee (my favorite). The other missionary and I could not believe it. Why were they offering food to us—overweight Americans—when they barely had anything? We wanted them to keep it, store it away, give it to the kids. We had breakfast bars and dried fruit in our suitcases. *Don't feed us!*

They wanted us to have it because they appreciated us and loved us. They saw having any food as a blessing and immediately distributed what little they had. We would have offended them by taking away their opportunity to bless us from their overflow. We blessed them by accepting their blessing to us.

That's quite a return policy.

No cup of coffee has ever made me feel more warm inside. It multiplied in my heart.

No matter how poor you are, or think you are, you can give out of the overflow. That overflow will mean more to God than anything given out of wealth.

Giving above and beyond reveals the heart of the giver. God gives more because he loves us more. He loves us to total satisfaction and beyond. God has leftover love.

GOD HAS LEFTOVER LOVE. Remember, leftovers taste good the second time, but they spoil if they sit around too long. What are you going to do with *your* remainders?

The Promise of Blessing

God pours handfuls and bucketfuls of blessings into our lives. We don't just get exactly what we need or the recommended daily allowance—we get overflow.

> You prepare a table before me
>   in the presence of my
>   enemies.
> You anoint my head with oil;
>   my cup overflows.

PSALM 23:5

Persecution? Setbacks? Enemies surrounding you? God overflows your cup.

> May the God of hope fill you with all joy and peace as you trust in him, so that you may overflow with hope by the power of the Holy Spirit.
> ROMANS 15:13

Dead ends? Feeling lost? Hopeless? The Holy Spirit multiplies his power in you so that you have enough joy and peace for yourself and an overflow that spills into others.

> Now may our God and Father himself and our Lord Jesus clear the way for us to come to you. May the Lord make your love increase and overflow for each other and for everyone else, just as ours does for you.
> 1 THESSALONIANS 3:11-12

Enemies? Feeling alone? Friendless? Unconnected? Detached? God loves you, and he makes love for others increase in your heart.

> Brothers and sisters, we want you to know about the grace that God has given the Macedonian churches. In the midst of a very severe trial, their overflowing joy and their extreme poverty welled up in rich generosity. For I testify that they gave as much as they were able, and even beyond their ability.
> 2 CORINTHIANS 8:1-3

How much can you give? Are you really too poor? God will multiply your generosity and joy when you give beyond what you are able. Paul knew the Macedonian churches had faced severe trials, and still they were able to give to his efforts.

God *rounds up* (another math term) the blessings in our lives. God makes sure we always have more than enough.

The promise of abundant blessings comes to us in so many ways, not just money and material goods. Look for them. Journal them. Be thankful for all blessings, large and small.

God multiplies the blessings in our lives over and above what we deserve. It's called *grace*. That blessing of grace compels us to gracefully bless. The more we bless, the more we are blessed.

> [Remember] the words the Lord Jesus himself said: "It is more blessed to give than to receive."
> ACTS 20:35

Such is the mystical mathematics of God.

Saying Grace

Lord, thank you for multiplying yourself in my life. You are a God who adds, multiplies, and overflows blessings to me. I want to reveal that love to others by doing the same. Show me where I need to go and overflow.

He makes grass grow for the cattle,
and plants for people to cultivate—
bringing forth food from the earth:
wine that gladdens human hearts,
oil to make their faces shine,
and bread that sustains their hearts.

PSALM 104:14-15

BREAD OF LIFE

The Promise of Eternity

Jesus declared, "I am the bread of life."

JOHN 6:35

I ONCE WORKED on an infomercial that dealt with a cooking product. After asking a number of great chefs to appear as the spokesman (Emeril turned us down before he became so noteworthy), we settled on a chef who had a small syndicated show and had written a couple of books. He wasn't the most popular chef around, but he had credentials and wanted more notoriety.

The man was larger than life. Loud voice. A comical accent. An infectious, Santa Claus–like laugh. You could tell he was someone. These kinds of people always get TV shows.

The director, producer, and I flew to Boston to meet him. One of the highlights on our agenda was lunch at what I figured would be one of the finest restaurants in town. You don't take a renowned chef to Taco Bell for Nachos BellGrande, right? As a starving writer, the greatest perks in my line of work are the lunch and dinner meetings. They're always free for me, and they're always at the best places around—places I could never afford to take my wife. If she's lucky, she gets a doggie bag, but she doesn't hold her breath.

So there I was in Boston with a TV-personality chef, sitting at the table, holding a menu with no prices. You could tell the waiters, the host, and the owner were getting nervous. Either they were informed about this chef's notoriety, or someone there recognized him. I watched people fall over themselves to make our meal more pleasant.

The food came out. My fork stabbed at the pasta before the waiter could set the plate down. This was going to be awesome. I could not wait.

Then I noticed the chef eyeing his steak with what I would call . . . contempt. He surveyed it on all sides. Probed it with his fork. Cut a piece with his knife. Then he dropped his utensils with a clank and motioned to the waiter.

"Tell the chef this steak is unacceptable. It must be cooked another five minutes."

The waiter apologized profusely.

I looked at my pasta, wondering if it really was as good as my first ten bites told me it was. Maybe I should send it back. Maybe I should just power through.

The owner sauntered up to the chef. "I am very sorry, sir. Your food will be out in just a moment. My humblest apologies."

The chef made it seem like no big deal. He understood, waving it off.

I began to slow down because our great, grand guest was eating nothing, and I had been shoveling it in like a recently released prisoner of war.

Finally, his food arrived, and the chef prepared to eat. After one bite, you could tell it wasn't right again. He signaled the waiter.

"Not quite it. Tell him it needs more sauce."

I could not believe it. I didn't think you could do that. My experience of dining came from my mom. You ate what she put in front of you, and you liked it!

Can you imagine . . . "Mother, these green peas are undercooked. Unacceptable! Another two minutes!"

I can just see that same plate of green peas sitting on my lap.

The waiter returned to the kitchen. Now I was one bite away from finishing my meal, so I scarfed down bread and drank water. For some reason, I was embarrassed that I liked the food.

The plate returned, this time with the restaurant's head chef. He bowed, apologized, nearly committed hara-kiri on the table, and made excuses about something only chefs understand.

Our chef was very cordial. He himself once worked in a restaurant and knew the demands placed upon these guys wearing the tall white hats. One of those demands includes wearing tall white hats.

Our chef took a big bite of steak. We all watched, sitting on the edges of our seats. Would he like it?

Suddenly he let out a tremendous *GAGGGG*! He dropped his utensils. Now, I was thinking, *This is a little extreme. If you don't like the food, just don't eat it. But to make a vomit sound that rocks the restaurant? That's just arrogant.*

However, I quickly realized that his hands were clasped around his own throat. *That's the universal sign for "I'm choking!"* I brilliantly deduced.

His face turned bright red. His mouth opened as he tried to breathe. For five seconds, nobody moved, everyone wondering the same thing I was: *Is he insulting the chef or choking to death?*

I jumped from my seat and began to move toward him. My mind was racing . . . *Heimlich, Heimlich, Heimlich . . . Fist below the abdomen . . . Or is it two fingers? . . . What is the abdomen? . . . Push in and up . . . How do you spell* Heimlich? . . .[1]

By the time I got to him, he had successfully dislodged the piece of steak from his esophagus and coughed it up on his plate.

The room let out a sigh of relief.

Frightened and embarrassed, the chef pushed the plate away. He didn't feel much like eating.

That last bite could have been his last.

As surreal and comical as that whole scene was, it gave me a glimpse into the world of chefs and restaurants. Today, chefs are as important to the selling of food as the food itself. Names such as Emeril Lagasse, Rachael Ray, Alton Brown, Bobby Flay, Gordon Ramsay, and Wolfgang Puck sell products ranging from television shows to cookbooks to frozen foods to restaurant cuisine.

An entire cable channel, Food Network, gives us a chance to see and learn from the experts themselves. Camera crews enter the sanctuary of culinary delight—the kitchen—to witness these virtuosos in action.

Restaurants are often designed with open kitchens so patrons can watch chefs in action as they prepare their food, turning these people into stage thespians. Benihana chefs perform as much as they prepare our food.

It appears we all want to meet the men and women who excel in providing us with the best food. We want to witness them at work, see their techniques, and enjoy their personalities. Because of their culinary know-how, they have become heroes and celebrities. Their willingness to step into the limelight suggests that these five-star chefs want us to know them.

One of the finest restaurants at Walt Disney World is Victoria & Albert's at Disney's Grand Floridian resort. (I'm hoping this shameless plug gets me a free meal for two . . . preferably on my anniversary in March.) This upscale adventure in fine dining serves only dinner. Each table has its own waiter, and there is only one seating a night. The reservation list is packed for months.

In the kitchen sits another table—the Chef's Table. Here the occupants receive special treatment (for a price). The chef himself sits down, talks to you, finds out what you like, then prepares a special dish to your liking. You like pasta? He makes the best pasta dish you've ever tasted. You like fish? He'll make a salmon that'll blow you out of the water. You like steak? No way you'll choke on his.

What an honor to dine in the presence of greatness, at the best table in the best restaurant, while the top chef sits down and asks for your order.

"The chef wants to meet me and cook for me? Wow."

Think of it—there is a chef out there who wants to cook you an extravagant meal and serve the best food you've ever had!

For a price.

When Jesus saw the hungry looks on the faces of the five thousand / four thousand, he wanted to make dinner for them. Good chefs want to feed people. It's in their blood. They want to serve and bless people through their creations.

Jesus was the head chef for the Feedings of the Five Thousand and Four Thousand. His purpose was not only to fill the stomachs of thousands of people but also to introduce himself to them in a very open kitchen. The fish sandwiches served by the head chef opened the people's minds to the power and character of God. If Jesus made thousands of fish sandwiches appear out of nowhere, is there anything he couldn't do?

Jesus introduced himself to myriads by serving up a recipe he still serves hungry souls today. He wanted people to meet him in a new and satisfying way and ultimately taste the best promise he had to offer . . .

Eternity.

The Bread of Life

There's a saying—"It's the best thing since sliced bread!" In 1928, the Chillicothe Baking Company, located outside Kansas City, started selling sliced bread and claimed in an ad that it was the "greatest forward step in the baking industry since bread was wrapped."[2] The introduction of sliced bread changed everything, especially the lives of busy homemakers.

Let's go to Capernaum, home to Peter and the ministry headquarters for Jesus and his disciples,[3] where Jesus is about to talk about bread. It's after the Feeding of the Five Thousand, and Jesus stood in the synagogue, surrounded by hard-line, conservative Jews accusing him of blasphemy. Jesus tried to convince the crowd that he was the best thing since the miracle bread he multiplied.

> Jesus answered, "Very truly I tell you, you are looking for me, not because you saw the signs I performed but because you ate the loaves and had your fill. Do not work for food that spoils, but for food that endures to eternal life, which the Son of Man will give you. For on him God the Father has placed his seal of approval."
> JOHN 6:26-27

That means some Pharisees were present at the Feeding of the Five Thousand. They saw the miraculous explosion of food, but they only saw the bread as sustenance to fill stomachs, not a miracle proving Jesus' deity. Jesus told them to stop looking at the surface. He was saying, "Think. What is the deeper meaning here?"

Jesus wanted them to know that it's not about the food or the money that buys the food or the work that gets the money to buy the food. All that stuff deteriorates. The real food is that which sustains a person for eternity. The person who provides that food is the Son of Man, who was sent by God. It's of him, by him, and through him.

This got their attention. And the questions started flowing . . .

Then they asked him, "What must we do to do the works God requires?"

Jesus answered, "The work of God is this: to believe in the one he has sent."

JOHN 6:28-29

Good ol' Pharisees. These religious leaders were all about religion, not relationship. They thought they needed to earn God's love instead of receiving it freely. First thing out of their mouths: Show us Five Steps to a Love Relationship with God or Ten Steps to Getting More Bread in Your Life. For them, God's commandments were not enough, so over time they lived by rules. It's all about "doing" for these guys.

"To eat this food, we must work—right, Jesus? Surely this food requires some intense labor." "No," Jesus replied. "All you have to do is believe." He made it clear who they must believe in—the one God has sent. The chef. The one who cooked up the meal of bread and fish. For some, that will be harder to do, but the same result comes to everyone who believes the one God has sent—they will receive what they need for eternal life.

The Pharisees then understood that Jesus was calling himself the Great Master Chef.

> So they asked him, "What sign then will you give
> that we may see it and believe you? What will you do?
> Our ancestors ate the manna in the wilderness; as it is
> written: 'He gave them bread from heaven to eat.'"
> JOHN 6:30-31

The group challenged Jesus: "So, what are you going to do? Show us your God power right now."

Jesus reminded them, "Didn't you just see the buffet I served?"

Jesus indicated that they had seen the miracle of the mass feeding and even eaten the bread. Now they had forgotten?

Many do not care about the past amazing feats God has done. Some people can list miracle upon miracle that God has performed, hear testimony after testimony of God's power to transform, and then just nod their heads and say, "That's nice, but what has he done for me lately?"

God is the same yesterday, today, and tomorrow.[4] What he did in the past is what he can do now. Who he was then is who he is now.

While displeased at their stubbornness, Jesus was pleased that this conversation was going precisely where he wanted it to go:

> Jesus said to them, "Very truly I tell you, it is not Moses
> who has given you the bread from heaven, but it is my

Father who gives you the true bread from heaven. For the bread of God is the bread that comes down from heaven and gives life to the world."

JOHN 6:32-33

The foundation for the symbolism grew.

As the Israelites had journeyed into the desert with God in the Old Testament, this New Testament crowd was journeying to a remote place with Jesus so they could hear him speak. Traveling to remote places obviously makes people hungry. In many ways, this world is a desert of dry ideas and unquenchable desires. Living here makes people thirsty and hungry.

We all want some real food.

Here Jesus drew the parallel between the God of the Old Testament who fed the Israelites in the desert and the God of the New Testament who fed the Jews (and later, Gentiles) in the wilderness. "Whatever your ancestors got from God in the old days, you can receive those same things from me today. I and the Father are one."[5] If God the Father made bread appear and Jesus made bread appear, then Jesus and God the Father are one. Right? Make sense?

Oh, it made sense, and Jesus probably caused hairs to stand up on the necks of the religious leaders when he said, "It is not Moses who has given you the bread from heaven."[6] Moses was their Captain America, Martin Luther King Jr., and Billy Graham all wrapped up in one. With this statement, Jesus knocked Moses down a notch below himself. Moses was merely a conduit and not the source.

Jesus had set them up for the big revelation. "When we talk about bread, we are talking about a spiritual life-giver.[7] As the manna fell from heaven in the past and the bread appeared in those baskets from heaven just a day ago, so is the manner in which *another bread* came from heaven and appeared on earth in the form of a man."

Whole-grain bread gives you life because it feeds your physical body. Spiritual bread does the same thing. It feeds your soul. Everyone who eats it receives eternal life.

Jesus whetted their appetite for more information.

"Sir," they said, "always give us this bread."
JOHN 6:34

Who wouldn't want to eat this kind of bread? Bread from God. Bread that gives life. They loved the proposition but hated the response.

Then Jesus declared, "I am the bread of life. Whoever comes to me will never go hungry, and whoever believes in me will never be thirsty. But as I told you, you have seen me and still you do not believe. All those the Father gives me will come to me, and whoever comes to me I will never drive away. For I have come down from heaven not to do my will but to do the will of him who sent me. And this is the will of him who sent me, that I shall lose none of all those he has given me, but raise them up at the last day. For my Father's will is that everyone who looks to the Son and believes in him shall have eternal life, and I will raise them up at the last day."
JOHN 6:35-40

That bread Jesus talked about . . . the manna in the desert, the bread used to feed the five thousand and the four thousand

. . . and the bread he later broke at the Lord's Supper . . . Jesus meant for it to represent himself. He is the bread. Not just the supplier and manufacturer, but the product itself.

All the promises God offers—attention, compassion, provision, spiritual health, power, community, fulfillment, blessing—come to us when we consume the bread: taking, receiving, and ingesting Jesus Christ into our lives.

Jesus used the Feeding of the Fish Sandwiches to represent the distribution and consumption of himself. He is the eternal Bread of Life.

Eight Essential Ingredients

On the side of many packages of store-bought bread, you can read the ingredients and promises for good nutrition. The product often promises to build healthy bodies by providing part of a recommended daily allowance of vitamins and iron. Wonder Bread boasted that it helped bodies in eight ways.[8]

According to Jesus' words in John 6:53-58, the label on the side of his bread lists eight essential reasons for eating it:

1. *Truth*: "Jesus said to them, 'Very truly I tell you.'"[9] You can trust this bread. There is no falsehood in it.

2. *Life*: "Unless you eat the flesh of the Son of Man and drink his blood, you have no life in you." Your heart may be beating, but this bread offers true, meaningful life.

3. *Resurrection*: "Whoever eats my flesh and drinks my blood has eternal life, and I will raise them up at the last day." This bread is so good for you that it promises to raise you up when you die.

4. *Authenticity*: "For my flesh is real food and my blood is real drink." The ingredients are organic, with no by-products or fillers. It's 100 percent whole.

5. *Relationship*: "Whoever eats my flesh and drinks my blood remains in me, and I in them." The bread keeps you in touch with its manufacturer.

6. *God*: "Just as the living Father sent me and I live because of the Father, so the one who feeds on me will live because of me." The owner of the company that makes this bread is God.

7. *Heaven*: "This is the bread that came down from heaven." The location of this company is heaven, not the world.

8. *Eternity*: "Your ancestors ate manna and died, but whoever feeds on this bread will live forever." The health benefits of this bread are eternal. It guarantees you will never die.

Why would anyone not want this miraculous bread? Well, sadly, Jesus listed these reasons because some had refused it.

> The Jews there began to grumble about him because he said, "I am the bread that came down from heaven." They said, "Is this not Jesus, the son of Joseph, whose father and mother we know? How can he now say, 'I came down from heaven'?"
> JOHN 6:41-42

Sometimes, when Jesus spoke symbolically, the people missed his point. In this case, they got the bread symbolism right away—Jesus had just said he came directly from heaven. "How can some human, born of earthly parents, be God?" they countered. The idea of God coming in human form hindered some from becoming believers . . . then and now.

> "Stop grumbling among yourselves," Jesus answered.
> "No one can come to me unless the Father who sent me
> draws them, and I will raise them up at the last day. It
> is written in the Prophets: 'They will all be taught by
> God.' Everyone who has heard the Father and learned
> from him comes to me. No one has seen the Father
> except the one who is from God; only he has seen the
> Father."
> JOHN 6:43-46

Left on our own, we will not seek God. God has to draw us to him, as the smell of fresh bread draws us to the bakery. The promise of spiritual nutrition catches the attention of many. The manufacturer advertises bread so that hearers will purchase the item. Those who ignore it find other means of nourishment. God advertises his bread on a regular basis. Are people listening? Are you?

> Very truly I tell you, the one who believes has eternal life.
> I am the bread of life. Your ancestors ate the manna in
> the wilderness, yet they died. But here is the bread that
> comes down from heaven, which anyone may eat and not
> die. I am the living bread that came down from heaven.
> Whoever eats this bread will live forever. This bread is my
> flesh, which I will give for the life of the world.
> JOHN 6:47-51

Bread of Life. Not store-bought wheat bread that gives you life for a few days, but a supernatural bread that gives life for eternity.

The Master Chef is offering—so take it and eat.

Eat Up

The Greek word translated as "eat" is *phago*. It means to consume food; however, it can be used figuratively or literally.[10] Obviously, Jesus didn't want the people to take a bite out of his arm. It's a figurative statement—symbolism again. He's saying, "Consume me completely, place my being into you, devour me spiritually, receive the eternal health benefits from my Word."

Jesus wants us to receive him into our lives—wholly, passionately, ravenously—and receive all the benefits that are found right on the label.

> Then the Jews began to argue sharply among themselves, "How can this man give us his flesh to eat?"
> JOHN 6:52

Jesus attempted, once again, to make it clear to those who were confused:

> Jesus said to them, "Very truly I tell you, unless you eat the flesh of the Son of Man and drink his blood, you have no life in you. Whoever eats my flesh and drinks my blood has eternal life, and I will raise them up at the last day. For my flesh is real food and my blood is real drink. Whoever eats my flesh and drinks my blood

remains in me, and I in them. Just as the living Father sent me and I live because of the Father, so the one who feeds on me will live because of me. This is the bread that came down from heaven. Your ancestors ate manna and died, but whoever feeds on this bread will live forever." He said this while teaching in the synagogue in Capernaum.

JOHN 6:53-59

Feed on me, Jesus begs. Don't feast on the things of this world that only weigh you down and make you fat. Fill your bodies with God.

When we dine on Jesus, we ingest his words, his sacrifice, his teaching, his promises, his commandments, and his love. He gives us health, vitality, enthusiasm, security, and life.

Jesus offered this menu to the Pharisees in the synagogue and to everyone who ate at the fish-sandwich buffets. "Choose me," he cried.

But what about you? Where are you dining? Do you consume the things of this world or the God of heaven? Are you hungry for something real, something wholesome, something essential for your well-being?

Jesus fills your hunger.

Jesus quenches your thirst.

Jesus is the one who can take care of all your needs.

Jesus does not play favorites; he loves everyone equally.

Jesus can turn nothing into something.

Jesus always gives us what's "good" for us.

Jesus gives us more than we need, in plentiful abundance.

Jesus can do the impossible.

Jesus wants to meet you and have a personal, deep, loving relationship with you. He will never turn you away.

Jesus multiplies the blessings in our lives.

Jesus will bring you back to life.

Jesus will give you eternal life.

Why would you go anywhere else to eat?

The Promise of Eternity

No matter how desperate my life seems, no matter how repetitive it becomes, no matter how many times I worry about the future, I know this . . . I have eternal life. This truth fills me because it promises that God loves me. It promises that I am forgiven. It promises that God will take care of me. It promises that God wants me to be with him forever.

It's the ultimate fish sandwich.

It's all I need to know when the hunger pains set in. This world may serve me a plate of cold bologna and cheese, but this is not the meal I will be eating for eternity. God promises a banquet in heaven with food prepared especially by him . . . the Master Chef.

GOD PROMISES THAT ONE DAY IN HEAVEN, HE WILL TAKE CARE OF ALL OUR PHYSICAL HURTS AND NEEDS IN AN ETERNAL ACT OF COMPASSION.

He promises that one day in heaven, he will take care of all our physical hurts and needs in an eternal act of compassion:

I heard a loud voice from the throne saying, "Look! God's dwelling place is now among the people, and he will dwell with them. They will be his people, and God himself will be with them and be their God. 'He will wipe every tear from their eyes.

There will be no more death' or mourning or crying or pain, for the old order of things has passed away."

REVELATION 21:3-4

Jesus will be the only item on the menu in heaven, and we'll get more and more of him each day. Each day, he will multiply himself in our hearts, and we won't be able to get enough:

"Never again will they hunger;
    never again will they thirst.
The sun will not beat down on them,"
    nor any scorching heat.
For the Lamb at the center of the throne
    will be their shepherd;
"he will lead them to springs of living water."
    "And God will wipe away every tear from their eyes."

REVELATION 7:16-17

Does that not fill your heart?
Don't you want that right now?
Come to Jesus with an appetite. He will fill you up.

[Jesus said,] "Here I am! I stand at the door and knock. If anyone hears my voice and opens the door, I will come in and eat with that person, and they with me."

REVELATION 3:20

My celebrity chef almost took his last bite on this earth. By coughing up the steak, he escaped death that time. But next time he approaches death's door, I wonder . . . *Where will he be dining for eternity?*

There is a price for this eternal bread from above. All bread comes at a price. While the bread is free in terms of dollars, it did cost in terms of sacrifice. Jesus sacrificed everything—his body, his blood, his life—to serve you the promises of this fish-sandwich buffet; what price must we pay to receive this meal?

You must realize that the measly meals served by this world pale in comparison to the eternal food of life offered by God. You must put aside your meal plans and seek God's plan. You cannot eat alone any longer.

If you want to dine with Jesus, all you have to do is invite him to the table. Jesus promises to come into your life and eat with you.

There's another saying—"You are what you eat." That's so true when it comes to Christ. You become one with Jesus as you consume him.

IF YOU WANT TO DINE WITH JESUS, ALL YOU HAVE TO DO IS INVITE HIM TO THE TABLE.

His life becomes your life.

His dreams become your dreams.

His plans become your plans.

If your diet consists of God's fish sandwiches, you will become filled with hopes and promises from the lessons learned during the Feeding of the Five Thousand.

Are you hungry?

Are you ready to eat?

Dig in.

Lord, I thank you for introducing yourself to me and serving me a meal that leads to eternal life. I thank you, Jesus, for offering yourself as a sacrifice for my sins so that I can consume you and receive you into my life. Jesus, you are the only way, the only truth, the only path to eternal life. I am hungry for you! I hear your knocking at the door of my heart and invite you in. I want only to consume the promises of God. I reject the junk food of this world and accept the essential ingredients of a relationship with you. I look forward to dining with you forever.

[Jesus said,] "Take and eat; this is my body. . . .
Drink from it, all of you. . . . This
is my blood of the covenant."

MATTHEW 26:26-28

COMMUNION

"Take and Eat"

AFTER YOU EAT your main course, traditionally, you get dessert. Some would say this course is the best part of the meal.

Some months after the fish-sandwich feedings, Jesus sat down for another meal, his last supper before the Cross. During the meal, he served bread and wine, what we call *Communion* today, the ideal conclusion (dessert) to our entire discussion.

> While they were eating, Jesus took bread, and when he
> had given thanks, he broke it and gave it to his disciples,
> saying, "Take and eat; this is my body."
>   Then he took a cup, and when he had given thanks,
> he gave it to them, saying, "Drink from it, all of you.
> This is my blood of the covenant, which is poured out
> for many for the forgiveness of sins. I tell you, I will
> not drink from this fruit of the vine from now on until

that day when I drink it new with you in my Father's kingdom."

MATTHEW 26:26-29

What Jesus talked about symbolically in John 6 he began to do literally in the next twelve (very important) hours from this moment to the Cross.

After immersing ourselves in the fish-sandwich feedings, we can't help but see similarities between their events and Communion:

- giving thanks to God, the source, before eating;
- the breaking and passing of bread one to another;
- the nutritional value of taking this bread;
- the blessing of forgiveness;
- the overflowing of love;
- the promise of future fulfillment;
- the consumption of Jesus himself; and
- the promise of eternity for all who take and eat.

The fish sandwiches involved more than just bread and fish. Communion is also more than just a menu of bread and wine.

The fish sandwiches represented Jesus ("I am the bread"). Communion represents his body, broken for you.

The fish sandwiches showed the extent of God's compassion and his attention to your needs. Communion shows the full extent God will go to—death—so that he can dine with his people.

The fish sandwiches interconnected thousands of people, unifying them as they served one another. Communion signifies unity, an interconnected relationship between all of us—the church—and Christ.

The fish sandwiches spoke of eternity for the ones who

allowed Christ to come into their lives. Communion does the same. Jesus promises that future meal to all believers, when he will lift his cup in celebration with those who have overcome.

I pray that this book gives you solid reasons to either begin a relationship with God or strengthen your relationship with God.

God is attentive to your life: He feels compassion for you, provides his resources, gives you the best he has to offer (his power, community), and blesses you, filling you with contentment for eternity.

Take and eat the promises God serves up to you today, and you'll never go hungry again.

Saying Grace

God, I delight in receiving your promises. They are so abundant. You take care of me and notice me amid everything going on in the world. You truly show compassion to me, even though I don't deserve it, and then you ask me to show that compassion to others. You are a God who can turn nothing into something. Thank you for giving what is good for me, even though I may not understand it at the time.

Lord, you bless me to overflowing, with more than I can handle, so I can spill over into the lives of others. You love to do the impossible, and I know you can do that in my life today. I want to know you in a deeper, more intimate way. Show me how you want me to serve others and return the blessing to my community. Thank you for multiplying what little I have. I'm truly fulfilled.

I look forward to eternity, when I'll get to know you and love you more. Jesus, you are the Bread of Life. I long to consume more of you.

THE FEEDING OF
THE FIVE THOUSAND

Matthew 14:15–21

As evening approached, the disciples came to him and said, "This is a remote place, and it's already getting late. Send the crowds away, so they can go to the villages and buy themselves some food."

Jesus replied, "They do not need to go away. You give them something to eat."

"We have here only five loaves of bread and two fish," they answered.

"Bring them here to me," he said. And he directed the people to sit down on the grass. Taking the five loaves and the two fish and looking up to heaven, he gave thanks and broke the loaves. Then he gave them to the disciples, and the disciples gave them to the people. They all ate and were satisfied, and the disciples picked up twelve basketfuls of broken pieces that were left over. The number of those who ate was about five thousand men, besides women and children.

Mark 6:35-44

By this time it was late in the day, so his disciples came to him. "This is a remote place," they said, "and it's already very late. Send the people away so that they can go to the surrounding countryside and villages and buy themselves something to eat."

But he answered, "You give them something to eat."

They said to him, "That would take more than half a year's wages! Are we to go and spend that much on bread and give it to them to eat?"

"How many loaves do you have?" he asked. "Go and see."

When they found out, they said, "Five—and two fish."

Then Jesus directed them to have all the people sit down in groups on the green grass. So they sat down in groups of hundreds and fifties. Taking the five loaves and the two fish and looking up to heaven, he gave thanks and broke the loaves. Then he gave them to his disciples to distribute to the people. He also divided the two fish among them all. They all ate and were satisfied, and the disciples picked up twelve basketfuls of broken pieces of bread and fish. The number of the men who had eaten was five thousand.

Luke 9:12-17

Late in the afternoon the Twelve came to him and said, "Send the crowd away so they can go to the surrounding villages and countryside and find food and lodging, because we are in a remote place here."

He replied, "You give them something to eat."

They answered, "We have only five loaves of bread and two fish—unless we go and buy food for all this crowd." (About five thousand men were there.)

But he said to his disciples, "Have them sit down in groups of about fifty each." The disciples did so, and everyone sat down. Taking the five loaves and the two fish and looking up to heaven, he gave thanks and broke them. Then he gave them to the disciples to distribute to the people. They all ate and were satisfied, and the disciples picked up twelve basketfuls of broken pieces that were left over.

John 6:1–13

Some time after this, Jesus crossed to the far shore of the Sea of Galilee (that is, the Sea of Tiberias), and a great crowd of people followed him because they saw the signs he had performed by healing the sick. Then Jesus went up on a mountainside and sat down with his disciples. The Jewish Passover Festival was near.

When Jesus looked up and saw a great crowd coming toward him, he said to Philip, "Where shall we buy bread for these people to eat?" He asked this only to test him, for he already had in mind what he was going to do.

Philip answered him, "It would take more than half a year's wages to buy enough bread for each one to have a bite!"

Another of his disciples, Andrew, Simon Peter's brother, spoke up, "Here is a boy with five small barley loaves and two small fish, but how far will they go among so many?"

Jesus said, "Have the people sit down." There was plenty of grass in that place, and they sat down (about five thousand men were there). Jesus then took the loaves, gave thanks, and distributed to those who were seated as much as they wanted. He did the same with the fish.

When they had all had enough to eat, he said to his disciples, "Gather the pieces that are left over. Let nothing be wasted." So they gathered them and filled twelve baskets with the pieces of the five barley loaves left over by those who had eaten.

THE FEEDING OF
THE FOUR THOUSAND

Matthew 15:29–38

Jesus left there and went along the Sea of Galilee. Then
he went up on a mountainside and sat down. Great
crowds came to him, bringing the lame, the blind, the
crippled, the mute and many others, and laid them at
his feet; and he healed them. The people were amazed
when they saw the mute speaking, the crippled made
well, the lame walking and the blind seeing. And they
praised the God of Israel.

Jesus called his disciples to him and said, "I have
compassion for these people; they have already been
with me three days and have nothing to eat. I do not
want to send them away hungry, or they may collapse on
the way."

His disciples answered, "Where could we get enough
bread in this remote place to feed such a crowd?"

"How many loaves do you have?" Jesus asked.

"Seven," they replied, "and a few small fish."

He told the crowd to sit down on the ground. Then
he took the seven loaves and the fish, and when he

had given thanks, he broke them and gave them to the disciples, and they in turn to the people. They all ate and were satisfied. Afterward the disciples picked up seven basketfuls of broken pieces that were left over. The number of those who ate was four thousand men, besides women and children.

Mark 8:1–9

During those days another large crowd gathered. Since they had nothing to eat, Jesus called his disciples to him and said, "I have compassion for these people; they have already been with me three days and have nothing to eat. If I send them home hungry, they will collapse on the way, because some of them have come a long distance."

His disciples answered, "But where in this remote place can anyone get enough bread to feed them?"

"How many loaves do you have?" Jesus asked.

"Seven," they replied.

He told the crowd to sit down on the ground. When he had taken the seven loaves and given thanks, he broke them and gave them to his disciples to distribute to the people, and they did so. They had a few small fish as well; he gave thanks for them also and told the disciples to distribute them. The people ate and were satisfied. Afterward the disciples picked up seven basketfuls of broken pieces that were left over. About four thousand were present.

PROMISES FROM THE SCRIPTURES

Attention

[Moses said,] "The LORD himself goes before you and will be with you; he will never leave you nor forsake you. Do not be afraid; do not be discouraged."

DEUTERONOMY 31:8

The LORD will not reject his people;
    he will never forsake his inheritance.

PSALM 94:14

The poor and needy search for water,
    but there is none;
    their tongues are parched with thirst.
But I the LORD will answer them;
    I, the God of Israel, will not forsake them.

ISAIAH 41:17

[Jesus said,] "Go and make disciples of all nations, baptizing them in the name of the Father and of the Son and of the Holy Spirit, and teaching them to obey

everything I have commanded you. And surely I am
with you always, to the very end of the age."
MATTHEW 28:19-20

[Jesus said,] "Indeed, the very hairs of your head are all
numbered. Don't be afraid; you are worth more than
many sparrows."
LUKE 12:7

Blessing

The LORD will send a blessing on your barns and on
everything you put your hand to. The LORD your God
will bless you in the land he is giving you.
DEUTERONOMY 28:8

They feast on the abundance of your house;
    you give them drink from your river of
        delights.
PSALM 36:8

Your wife will be like a fruitful vine
    within your house;
your children will be like olive shoots
    around your table.
Yes, this will be the blessing
    for the man who fears the LORD.
PSALM 128:3-4

Honor the LORD with your wealth,
    with the firstfruits of all your crops;

then your barns will be filled to overflowing,
    and your vats will brim over with new wine.
PROVERBS 3:9-10

I will make them and the places surrounding my hill a
blessing. I will send down showers in season; there will
be showers of blessing.
EZEKIEL 34:26

"Bring the whole tithe into the storehouse, that there
may be food in my house. Test me in this," says the
LORD Almighty, "and see if I will not throw open the
floodgates of heaven and pour out so much blessing that
there will not be room enough to store it."
MALACHI 3:10

May the God of hope fill you with all joy and peace as
you trust in him, so that you may overflow with hope by
the power of the Holy Spirit.
ROMANS 15:13

Praise be to the God and Father of our Lord Jesus
Christ, who has blessed us in the heavenly realms with
every spiritual blessing in Christ.
EPHESIANS 1:3

Do not repay evil with evil or insult with insult. On the
contrary, repay evil with blessing, because to this you
were called so that you may inherit a blessing.
1 PETER 3:9

Mercy, peace and love be yours in abundance.
JUDE 1:2

Community

God said to him, "I am God Almighty; be fruitful and increase in number. A nation and a community of nations will come from you, and kings will be among your descendants."
GENESIS 35:11

A friend loves at all times,
    and a brother is born for a time of adversity.
PROVERBS 17:17

As iron sharpens iron,
    so one person sharpens another.
PROVERBS 27:17

Two are better than one,
    because they have a good return for their labor:
If either of them falls down,
    one can help the other up.
But pity anyone who falls
    and has no one to help them up.
Also, if two lie down together, they will keep warm.
    But how can one keep warm alone?
Though one may be overpowered,
    two can defend themselves.
A cord of three strands is not quickly broken.
ECCLESIASTES 4:9-12

[Jesus said,] "I tell you that you are Peter, and on this rock I will build my church, and the gates of Hades will not overcome it."
MATTHEW 16:18

[The believers] devoted themselves to the apostles' teaching and to fellowship, to the breaking of bread and to prayer. Everyone was filled with awe at the many wonders and signs performed by the apostles. All the believers were together and had everything in common. They sold property and possessions to give to anyone who had need. Every day they continued to meet together in the temple courts. They broke bread in their homes and ate together with glad and sincere hearts, praising God and enjoying the favor of all the people. And the Lord added to their number daily those who were being saved.
ACTS 2:42-47

Compassion

The LORD said, "I will cause all my goodness to pass in front of you, and I will proclaim my name, the LORD, in your presence. I will have mercy on whom I will have mercy, and I will have compassion on whom I will have compassion."
EXODUS 33:19

The LORD is compassionate and gracious,
    slow to anger, abounding in love.
PSALM 103:8

Shout for joy, you heavens;
    rejoice, you earth;
    burst into song, you mountains!
For the LORD comforts his people
    and will have compassion on his afflicted ones.
ISAIAH 49:13

Praise be to the God and Father of our Lord Jesus
Christ, the Father of compassion and the God of all
comfort, who comforts us in all our troubles, so that we
can comfort those in any trouble with the comfort we
ourselves receive from God.
2 CORINTHIANS 1:3-4

As you know, we count as blessed those who have
persevered. You have heard of Job's perseverance and
have seen what the Lord finally brought about. The Lord
is full of compassion and mercy.
JAMES 5:11

Eternity

Trust in the LORD forever,
    for the LORD, the LORD himself, is the Rock eternal.
ISAIAH 26:4

How great are his signs,
    how mighty his wonders!
His kingdom is an eternal kingdom;
    his dominion endures from generation to generation.
DANIEL 4:3

God so loved the world that he gave his one and only Son, that whoever believes in him shall not perish but have eternal life.

JOHN 3:16

Jesus answered, "Everyone who drinks this water will be thirsty again, but whoever drinks the water I give them will never thirst. Indeed, the water I give them will become in them a spring of water welling up to eternal life."

JOHN 4:13-14

Now this is eternal life: that they know you, the only true God, and Jesus Christ, whom you have sent.

JOHN 17:3

The wages of sin is death, but the gift of God is eternal life in Christ Jesus our Lord.

ROMANS 6:23

We fix our eyes not on what is seen, but on what is unseen, since what is seen is temporary, but what is unseen is eternal.

2 CORINTHIANS 4:18

May our Lord Jesus Christ himself and God our Father, who loved us and by his grace gave us eternal encouragement and good hope, encourage your hearts and strengthen you in every good deed and word.

2 THESSALONIANS 2:16-17

We know also that the Son of God has come and has
given us understanding, so that we may know him who
is true. And we are in him who is true by being in his
Son Jesus Christ. He is the true God and eternal life.
1 JOHN 5:20

Whoever has ears, let them hear what the Spirit says to
the churches. To the one who is victorious, I will give
the right to eat from the tree of life, which is in the
paradise of God.
REVELATION 2:7

Fulfillment

God is not human, that he should lie,
    not a human being, that he should change his mind.
Does he speak and then not act?
    Does he promise and not fulfill?
NUMBERS 23:19

Satisfy us in the morning with your unfailing love,
    that we may sing for joy and be glad all our days.
PSALM 90:14

I will bless her with abundant provisions;
    her poor I will satisfy with food.
PSALM 132:15

You open your hand
    and satisfy the desires of every living thing.
PSALM 145:16

This is what I have observed to be good: that it is appropriate for a person to eat, to drink and to find satisfaction in their toilsome labor under the sun during the few days of life God has given them—for this is their lot.

ECCLESIASTES 5:18

Why spend money on what is not bread,
    and your labor on what does not satisfy?
Listen, listen to me, and eat what is good,
    and you will delight in the richest of fare.

ISAIAH 55:2

The Lord will guide you always;
    he will satisfy your needs in a sun-scorched
        land
    and will strengthen your frame.
You will be like a well-watered garden,
    like a spring whose waters never fail.

ISAIAH 58:11

Power

He performs wonders that cannot be
        fathomed,
    miracles that cannot be counted.

JOB 5:9

You are the God who performs miracles;
    you display your power among the peoples.

PSALM 77:14

Remember the wonders he has done,
    his miracles, and the judgments he
        pronounced.

PSALM 105:5

How great are his signs,
    how mighty his wonders!
His kingdom is an eternal kingdom;
    his dominion endures from generation
        to generation.

DANIEL 4:3

Everyone was filled with awe at the many wonders and
signs performed by the apostles.

ACTS 2:43

Provision

Abraham called that place The LORD Will Provide. And
to this day it is said, "On the mountain of the LORD it
will be provided."

GENESIS 22:14

[God's Word to King David, as revealed to Nathan:]
"I have been with you wherever you have gone, and I
have cut off all your enemies from before you. Now I
will make your name like the names of the greatest men
on earth. And I will provide a place for my people Israel
and will plant them so that they can have a home of
their own and no longer be disturbed. Wicked people
will not oppress them anymore, as they did at the

beginning and have done ever since the time I appointed leaders over my people Israel. I will also subdue all your enemies.

"I declare to you that the LORD will build a house for you."

1 CHRONICLES 17:8-10

You provide a broad path for my feet,
    so that my ankles do not give way.

PSALM 18:36

[God's Word, as revealed to Jeremiah:] "[Jerusalem] will bring me renown, joy, praise and honor before all nations on earth that hear of all the good things I do for it; and they will be in awe and will tremble at the abundant prosperity and peace I provide for it."

JEREMIAH 33:9

[Barnabas and Paul said,] "[God] has not left himself without testimony: He has shown kindness by giving you rain from heaven and crops in their seasons; he provides you with plenty of food and fills your hearts with joy."

ACTS 14:17

For if, by the trespass of the one man, death reigned through that one man, how much more will those who receive God's abundant provision of grace and of the gift of righteousness reign in life through the one man, Jesus Christ!

ROMANS 5:17

Command those who are rich in this present world not to be arrogant nor to put their hope in wealth, which is so uncertain, but to put their hope in God, who richly provides us with everything for our enjoyment.

1 TIMOTHY 6:17

Spiritual Health

Do not be wise in your own eyes;
    fear the LORD and shun evil.
This will bring health to your body
    and nourishment to your bones.

PROVERBS 3:7-8

[God's Word, as revealed to Jeremiah:] "I will bring health and healing to [Jerusalem]; I will heal my people and will let them enjoy abundant peace and security."

JEREMIAH 33:6

[Jesus said,] "Seek first [your heavenly Father's] kingdom and his righteousness, and all these things will be given to you as well."

MATTHEW 6:33

NOTES

CHAPTER 1: HUNGRY?

1. *Mother Goose: The Old Nursery Rhymes* (Alcester, UK: Pook Press, 2013), n.p.
2. Author's paraphrase of Matthew 4:4.

CHAPTER 2: FEEDING THOUSANDS

1. The following description is a compilation of the accounts found in Matthew 14:15-21, Mark 6:35-44, Luke 9:12-17, and John 6:1-13.
2. "Tabgha—Church of the Multiplication of the Loaves and the Fishes," Consulate General of Israel to the Mid-Atlantic, December 19, 1999, http://embassies.gov.il/MFA/IsraelExperience/history/Pages/Tabgha-%20Church%20of%20the%20Multiplication%20of%20the%20Loaves.aspx.
3. "Tabgha," BiblePlaces.com, accessed August 27, 2018, https://www.bibleplaces.com/tabgha/.
4. "Church of the Primacy of Peter, Tabgha," Sacred Destinations, accessed August 27, 2018, http://www.sacred-destinations.com/israel/tabgha-church-of-primacy-of-peter.
5. The following is a compilation of the accounts found in Matthew 15:29-38 and Mark 8:1-9.
6. To read about Jesus healing the demon-possessed man, see Mark 5:1-20. For information about the area where this miracle occurred, see https://biblewalks.com/sites/kursi.html.
7. See Matthew 15:24.

CHAPTER 3: ATTENTION

1. Jasmin Tahmaseb-McConatha, "Comforting Third Spaces," *Psychology Today*, March 14, 2015, https://www.psychologytoday.com/us/blog/live-long-and-prosper/201503/comforting-third-spaces.
2. "Where Everybody Knows Your Name," music and lyrics by Gary Portnoy and Judy Hart (Angelo), copyright © 1982 by Addax Music Company, Inc.,

theme song to the television show *Cheers* (1982–1993), originally produced and directed by James Burrows (creator), original air date September 30, 1982.
3. See Romans 8:26.

CHAPTER 4: COMPASSION
1. "Tradition attributes the biblical letter to the man Paul calls 'James, the Lord's brother' (Galatians 1:19). James was probably the eldest of the four brothers named in Mark 6:3." *James*, LifeChange Bible Study series (Colorado Springs: NavPress, 2009), 9.
2. "The 10 Hungriest Countries in the World and How You Can Help Them," The Daily Meal, accessed June 29, 2018, https://www.thedailymeal.com /travel/10-hungriest-countries-world-and-how-you-can-help-them-0. For a more comprehensive list of the hungriest countries in 2014, see https://www .globalhungerindex.org/pdf/en/2014/posters.pdf.
3. David Berkowitz, "My Testimony," AriseandShine.org, accessed June 29, 2018, http://www.ariseandshine.org/testimony-translations.html.
4. "David Berkowitz—Son of Sam—44-Caliber Killer," True Crime & Justice, accessed June 29, 2018, http://www.karisable.com/skazberk.htm.

CHAPTER 5: BREAD, FISH, AND A BOY
1. Of the four Gospel accounts of this event, two mention the monetary cost of feeding five thousand people. Neither identifies an exact amount (see Mark 6:37 and John 6:7). Eight months' wages is used here for the purpose of the following illustration.
2. John 21:11 numbers the fish caught in the net at 153. This was as much as the net could handle. With nearly fifteen thousand to feed, it would require gathering one hundred similar nets full of fish for one fish per person.

CHAPTER 6: LOOKING UP
1. John is the only Gospel to omit this detail; see Matthew 14:19, Mark 6:41, and Luke 9:16.
2. Mignon Fogarty, "Swear Words in Text: Grawlixes, Maledicta, and More," Quick and Dirty Tips, May 15, 2009, https://www.quickanddirtytips.com /education/grammar/swear-words-in-text?page=1.
3. "Health Benefits of Whole Grains Confirmed," ScienceDaily, May 10, 2007, http://www.sciencedaily.com/releases/2007/05/070509161030.htm. Adapted from a Wake Forest University Baptist Medical Center study.
4. For an excellent resource on identifying whether foods are truly whole grain, see: "Identifying Whole Grain Products," Whole Grains Counsel, accessed October 30, 2018, https://wholegrainscouncil.org/whole-grains-101 /identifying-whole-grain-products.
5. "Fish and Your Health," Food Insight, October 8, 2012, last modified May 23, 2014, https://www.foodinsight.org/Fish_and_Your_Health.
6. See Exodus 12:8.

7. See Exodus 16 and Numbers 11:7-9.
8. See Jonah 1–2.
9. John Piper, "Bethlehem: House of Bread," Desiring God, April 28, 1981, https://www.desiringgod.org/articles/bethlehem-house-of-bread.
10. See Mark 1:17.
11. See, for example, Matthew 26:26.
12. See John 21:1-6.
13. See Matthew 17:24-27.
14. John 6:35.
15. Carolyn Gregoire, "New Year's Resolutions Are Bound to Fail. Try This Instead," HuffPost, December 28, 2016, last modified January 3, 2017, https://www.huffingtonpost.com/entry/new-years-resolutions-psychology_us_5862d599e4b0d9a59459654c.
16. K. Aleisha Fetters, "How Long Does It Really Take to Make Healthy Eating and Exercise a Habit?" *US News and World Report*, April 28, 2017, https://health.usnews.com/wellness/food/articles/2017-04-28/how-long-does-it-really-take-to-make-healthy-eating-and-exercise-a-habit.

CHAPTER 7: MIRACLE
1. To read more about the "Miracle on Ice," see "The 1980 U.S. Olympic Team," U.S. Hockey Hall of Fame, accessed October 16, 2018, https://www.ushockeyhalloffame.com/page/show/831562-the-1980-u-s-olympic-team.
2. Jessie Garcia, *Going for Wisconsin Gold: Stories of Our State Olympians* (Madison, WI: Wisconsin Historical Society Press, 2016), 102.
3. See Genesis 1.
4. See Exodus 14.
5. See Exodus 16:1-35, Exodus 17:1-7, and Numbers 20:1-13.
6. See Joshua 3–4.
7. See Joshua 6:1-20.
8. See Joshua 10:12-14.
9. See John 2:1-12.
10. See Matthew 17:24-27.
11. See, for example, Matthew 8:1-3 and Luke 17:11-19.
12. See, for example, Matthew 9:27-30, Matthew 20:29-34, Mark 8:22-26, and John 9:1-7.
13. See Luke 8:26-39.
14. See John 11:1-44 and Mark 5:21-43, respectively.
15. See John 6:16-21.
16. See Matthew 17:1-9.
17. See Luke 24:1-49.
18. See 2 Kings 4:38-44.
19. Not the guy who died and came back from the dead, thanks to Jesus.
20. See Luke 16:24.

21. Mike Celizic, "Rescuer: 'Lord Led Me' to Missing Girl," Today, June 25, 2010, https://www.today.com/news/rescuer-lord-led-me-missing-girl-wbna36497665.

CHAPTER 8: GROUPS OF FIFTY

1. See Genesis 2:18.
2. "The Names of God in the Old Testament," Blue Letter Bible, accessed August 27, 2018, https://www.blueletterbible.org/study/misc/name_god.cfm.
3. "Andy Stanley Says: Life Change Happens in Circles Not Rows - Andy Stanley," YouTube video, 2:21, posted by Dallas Theological Seminary, June 1, 2015, https://www.youtube.com/watch?v=2uuBEdR6r-0.

CHAPTER 9: SATISFIED

1. "(I Can't Get No) Satisfaction," words and music copyright © 1965, 1993 by Mick Jagger and Keith Richards.
2. Bible Hub, s.v. "chortazó," *Thayer's Greek Lexicon*, accessed July 25, 2018, http://biblehub.com/greek/5526.htm.
3. See Numbers 11 for the full account of what happened when the Israelites complained about their desert food options.
4. To learn more about this Star Trek phenomenon, see "Replicator," Fandom, accessed October 18, 2018, http://memory-alpha.wikia.com/wiki/Replicator.
5. "You Can't Always Get What You Want," words and music copyright © 1969, 1997 by Mick Jagger and Keith Richards.
6. Merriam-Webster.com, s.v. "need," accessed July 25, 2018, https://www.merriam-webster.com/dictionary/need.
7. Merriam-Webster.com, s.v. "want," accessed July 25, 2018, https://www.merriam-webster.com/dictionary/want.

CHAPTER 10: LEFTOVERS

1. "My Hero, Zero," words and music by Robert L. Dorough, copyright © 1971, 1999 by American Broadcasting Music, Inc. (PWH).
2. *It's the Great Pumpkin, Charlie Brown*, copyright © 1966, 1995 by United Feature Syndicate, Inc. (PWH), directed by Bill Melendez, written by Charles M. Schulz, aired October 27, 1966, on CBS. To watch the clip referenced in this chapter, see "It's the Great Pumpkin, Charlie Brown (1966) I Got A Rock . . . ," YouTube video, posted by MrKsummer7, October 20, 2011, https://www.youtube.com/watch?v=9EXpklvbrNk.
3. Tom Kuntz, "Word for Word/Billboards From God; Did Somebody Say, 'Give Me a Sign, Lord'?," *New York Times*, July 18, 1999, https://www.nytimes.com/1999/07/18/weekinreview/word-for-word-billboards-from-god-did-somebody-say-give-me-a-sign-lord.html.
4. These and other billboard messages from this ad campaign may be found in Kuntz, "Word for Word," and/or here: "About," GodSpeaks, accessed July 26, 2018, https://godspeaks.com/about/.
5. See Genesis 8:17; 9:7.

6. "multiplied greatly": See Exodus 1:7, 12, 20. "adopted them as his own": If possible, read the entire book of Exodus; if not, at least read Exodus 6:6-8.
7. See Acts 2:1-41.
8. Merriam-Webster.com, s.v. "X factor," accessed August 28, 2018, https://www.merriam-webster.com/dictionary/X%20factor.
9. "Heritage," TupperwareBrands, accessed February 13, 2012, https://tupperwarebrands.com/company/heritage.
10. Matthew 6:26.
11. The Parable of the Ten Minas; see Luke 19:11-26.
12. Luke 19 calls the unit of money a *mina*, which is three months' wages. If the average person makes $24,000 a year, that's $2,000 a month and $6,000 for three.

CHAPTER 11: BREAD OF LIFE

1. Hopefully, you'll never need to implement the Heimlich maneuver. It's a good idea to know the proper procedure to follow, though, just in case. See Mayo Clinic, "Choking: First Aid," accessed October 23, 2018, https://www.mayoclinic.org/first-aid/first-aid-choking/basics/art-20056637.
2. "The Origin of Bread and the Phrase 'The Best Thing Since Sliced Bread,'" Today I Found Out, May 5, 2014, http://www.todayifoundout.com/index.php/2014/05/origin-phrase-best-thing-since-sliced-bread-2/.
3. See Mark 2:1.
4. See Hebrews 13:8.
5. "Whatever your ancestors . . .": author's paraphrase of John 6:31-32, 48-49; "I and the Father are one": John 10:30.
6. John 6:32.
7. Author's paraphrase of John 6:33.
8. For more information about the eight health benefits of eating Wonder Bread (according to its maker), see "VINTAGE 1952 WONDER BREAD COMMERCIAL," YouTube video, posted by "TV TOY MEMORIES," October 15, 2012, https://www.youtube.com/watch?v=GEfWShkO4Ac.
9. The quotes in this list are drawn from John 6:53-58.
10. Bible Hub, s.v. "phago," *Strong's Exhaustive Concordance*, accessed July 30, 2018, http://biblehub.com/str/greek/5315.htm.

Our good friend Troy Schmidt has served up a delicious main course of God's promises—his miracles and power all in one. The Feeding of the Five Thousand is one of those miracles discussed but rarely dissected with the kind of humor and insight Troy brings to everything he does. Dine on this book—then bring your friends back for seconds!

DAVID AND JASON BENHAM, authors, entrepreneurs, speakers

The miracle of Jesus feeding the five thousand is one of my favorite stories. How fun it would have been to be there—I love to imagine the people's astonished joy and laughter as Jesus provided more and more and *more*. Troy Schmidt unpacks the miracle that offers far more than a feast of food. In Jesus' economy, there is always more and more and more.

TRICIA LOTT WILLIFORD, author of *You Can Do This*

If you are hungry for a book that will feed your soul . . . here you go! Eat up! *Fish Sandwiches* is chock-full of soul-satisfying truth! In this book, Troy Schmidt serves a well-written, practical, and humorous feast of God's promises that is sure to leave you spiritually full and even more confident that we serve a God who loves when we are well fed.

ARRON CHAMBERS, author of *Eats with Sinners*

Troy Schmidt has written an engaging and inspiring work that expounds on Jesus' miracle of the Feeding of the Five Thousand. You'll find your attention grabbed and your spirit raised as you follow his explanation and practical application of the various parts of this story. This two-thousand-year-old miracle met the people's needs then and can also meet our needs today.

TOM YEAKLEY, author of *Praying over God's Promises*